# TIME TO LIGHTEN THE FCK UP

## MADISON MALLOY

Copyright © 2022 by Madison Malloy

TIME TO LIGHTEN THE F*CK UP

Quantity sales and special discounts are available on quantity purchases by corporations, associations, and others. For details, contact the publisher at the address above.

Orders by U.S. trade bookstores and wholesalers. Email info@BeyondPublishing. net

The Beyond Publishing Speakers Bureau can bring authors to your live event. For more information or to book an event contact the Beyond Publishing Speakers Bureau speak@BeyondPublishing.net

Illustrations by Bob Eckstein

The Author can be reached directly at BeyondPublishing.net

Manufactured and printed in the United States of America distributed globally by BeyondPublishing.net

BEYOND
PUBLISHING

New York | Los Angeles | London | Sydney

ISBN Softcover: 978-1-63792-369-6

ISBN Hardcover: 978-1-63792-368-9

*This book is dedicated to my parents,*
*who believed in me before I even believed in myself.*

# CONTENTS

# TIME TO INTRODUCE MYSELF

Let me guess. You found this book in the "self help" section. It caught your attention because it has the f-word in the title. "Whoa, it's edgy!" Then, you saw my big ol'face on the cover, and you thought, "Right. This person Madison Malloy is going to *help me?*"

You thought, "Who is this chick, to think she knows how to make my life better? She looks like she would donate money to an animal shelter and then show up to the event wearing fur. She looks like a trophy wife whose biggest problem ever was when her border collie learned how to arc the electric fence and knocked up the neighbor's show labradoodle. What's she going to recommend: Cool-Sculpting, Lexapro, and the wine-of-the-month club? I'm supposed to believe that this girl, who looks like she's been so busy thumb-typing one-star Yelp reviews that she probably doesn't know Pluto isn't a planet anymore, can tell me how to fix my life?"

And does your life even need fixing?

Look, you're "adulting," right? You're doing the things you're supposed to do. You work, make money, meet people, date, fool around, make mistakes, make progress, call your folks, get fired, find something else, buy something nice, break up, get drunk, and work some more. Time passes, so you must be living because you're still here, waiting around, for life to suddenly go BOOM, and make perfect sense.

You were young, just…yesterday, wasn't it? Fresh out of college and bright-eyed and full of plans. You were gonna change the world, get rich, and get laid and/or married and "have it all." That meant making a name for yourself. Finding something to call happiness. Proving anyone who ever doubted you wrong.

But more and more, the days go on without the BOOM ever coming. And shit is so much harder and so much less satisfying than you thought it would be! Life feels like a frat party where you're sucking everybody's dick just so you'll get invited back next time. Problem is, every time, it's the same sausagefest. Like what's the solution? Where's the doorway? What's the secret sauce?

Okay, maybe you don't need *fixing*, but maybe you can still give me a chance to help you out, because I think I can.

Now, you may still be stuck on the fact that I look more likely to mistake you for the waiter than help you out. I get a lot of crap from people about my looks. It's one thing to be easy on the eyes. But genetics endowed me with a face that says, "I'd like to speak with your manager." I've even been told I look like a second wife (which I think means "*I don't want to have kids, but I'll vaguely give a shit about yours.*") and maybe, on first impressions, I kind of do. But that's because you don't know me.

And really, you don't have to get to know me. This book is not about me. If it were about me, it would be in the "biography" section. This book is about you.

"Okay," you're saying, "but Madison, you don't know me. And books are pretty much a one-way transaction, so you're not going to get to know me and so *how are you going to help me?*"

Here's how. It's classic. I've been through some shit. I've made some mistakes. I'm going to tell you about these mistakes, and then you can *not* make those same mistakes, and you'll thank me. Consider me the friend who tells you the truth, like when I told my friend that smoking would cause lines around her mouth. She said, "Sucking dicks does the same thing," and I said, "Touché, but I don't suck a pack of dicks a day. Want some gum?"

But with my experiences came this nugget of wisdom: most of the time, we are our own worst enemies and our own biggest obstacles. We absolutely must get out of our own way. As you're navigating life's labyrinth, your insecurity, fear, anger, resentment, and envy are going to cause you more trouble than just about anything else ever will, and they will hurt you more than they'll ever hurt anyone else. What's the best way to step out of your own way?

Time to lighten the fuck up.

Sure, I hear you. "Wow, thanks Madison. Problem solved. I've lightened the fuck up, and now, everything's better."

So, obviously there's more to it than a catchy, humorous, and rather brilliant self-help book title. Just because you lighten the fuck up doesn't mean you're about to catapult into a land of wealth and orgasms. Stick with me, and I'll tell you how this first step of lightening-the-fuck-up-ness will prepare you to:

- Stop living in scarcity and envy

- Understand what you want

- Understand why you want it

- See the multiple pathways toward getting it

- See opportunities unfolding before you

- Tell the Universe you are ready to receive

- Live in faith, abundance, and gratitude

- Recognize when obstacles are of your own making

- Clear obstacles out of your way

Let's clear your vision. Let's wipe the slate clean. Let's lighten the…

*Fucking* seriously? I just spent all this time saying that this book is not about me, and now I'm going to introduce myself and talk about my background including my childhood.

But there's this contractual thing: I must tell you at least a little bit about me because otherwise, it's shady. If I don't give you *some* information, my publisher might ask, "Um...should we just leave your name off the cover then?"

No way! Because I wanna keep making that money! The first thing you're going to learn about me is that I think money is awesome.

And good news - there's enough of it out there for all of us.

*****

I grew up in Denver, Colorado.

No, I don't know how to ski. Everyone who finds out I'm from Denver says, "Do you ski?" Which I guess I understand, because of the mountains and all, but I would never meet someone from New Jersey and lead with, "Do you dump bodies in the Hudson River?"

But, from the time I was making my Barbie hump Ken, I thought I knew what I wanted from life. All my little elementary school friends wanted to be vets, teachers, cowboys, ninjas, flight attendants, and one little boy said he wanted to be a stove. I just wanted to be a rich man's wife. I wanted that sparkling mansion, that big diamond ring, and a different bikini for every day of the year. I wanted to have nice shit all around me.

This sounds like I was raised in a poor home. You're always hearing about children who suffered poverty just dreaming of the day when they could have a Ferrari and a mink coat, but that was not the case for me. My parents were great. Dad was an accountant. We lived in a perfectly lovely home. I had everything I needed. Now, my folks didn't give me or my older brother everything we wanted because they didn't want us to be entitled little bitches, but I never lived with need.

I just seemed to live with a lot of wants, like "*I want what Barbie has!*" That silicone slut had everything - dream house, fancy car, all these clothes, and twenty-seven careers.

My older brother by two years teamed up with our same-age cousin to torment me through my formative years. Those boys were always ordering me around. I was their personal assistant, fetching and carrying and putting up with their shit all day long. They kept promising me a farting teddy bear – the cuddly, flatulent toy of my dreams – like somehow those two little shits were going to procure this Temple of Doom treasure for me so I could have let Barbie have a furry experience (it was only fair; she'd been humping a guy with a smooth crotch for years). Well, I *never* got my farting bear, but I got toughened up enough that I rarely put up with crap from anyone else.

I aspired for fame and greatness (i.e., money!). When I was a freshman in high school, I wanted to be the next Pam Anderson, running down the beach in slo-mo with my big ol' fake ta-tas barely moving. That was Barbie's world, come to life! But then my grandparents introduced me to Warren Buffett (not literally), and I fell in love with the whole concept of Wall Street.

My dad's parents were lovely people, but they were strict and a little intimidating. We only saw them a couple times a year because they had retired down in North Carolina. For some reason, it seemed important that I never disappoint them. I don't think I've ever tried so hard to impress anyone as my paternal grandparents. I remember telling my dad one time to lie about my grades, so they wouldn't think I was stupid.

Grandma and Grandpa weren't what you'd call "rich," but they had solid money skills – they knew how to save and invest, and were very comfortable in their later years. Grandma told me and my brother, "If you want to make it big in the business world, you must know how to play golf." They bestowed on us the crappiest set of golf clubs sold on the market – the Beggar's Choice Pseudo-Deluxe set, with the box that says, *"Don't waste your good money on those little brats"* – and told us, "Go down to the driving range, and don't come back until you can hit that ball. Because if you want to close a deal, you must be able to play golf." And that's how I learned to hitchhike.

At their lake house in the summer, we'd try to sneak in an episode of *Beavis and Butthead*, but they would say, "Enough of this. Crank up the CNBC." Grandpa watched the market constantly. He said, "Madison, you should be investing. Why aren't you playing the market?"

"Because I'm twelve."

"That's no excuse for not building your portfolio."

So, this was an early feeling I had – gotta make a shit ton of money! I no longer wanted to be Barbie – I wanted to own the 80-foot yacht that Barbie was trying to slut her way onto. I never wanted anyone telling me what I could and couldn't do. I wanted the luxury of complete financial freedom. I wanted bajillions and kazillions of dollars.

Oh, that Warren Buffett! He didn't have Pam Anderson's ta-tas, and he wasn't as funny as *Beavis and Butthead*, but he had *all* the money, and everybody kissed his ass and begged him to tell them what to do with *their* money, and *I wanted to be him.*

Everything I saw told me that a job on Wall Street could lay all that sweet money right at my feet. So, in a few short years,

I, a fresh-faced, starry-eyed college grad, landed a job at a Wall Street firm in New York City…

…in 2005.

And anyone who lived through those years knows exactly what was coming next.

# CHAPTER ONE

## TIME TO STOP CHASING THE MONEY

### *Why Do We Chase Money?*

Well, duh! Seems like there's an obvious answer to this question. We chase the money because we need it to survive. Without money, we can't eat. We don't have shelter. We can't get the things we need. If you don't think money is important, try living without it. When you're searching your couch cushions to find enough change to buy a coffee, you start seeing the value of money real fast.

But that's not the type of money that we're talking about in this chapter, and "earning a living" is not the same as "chasing."

I love money. It has this beautiful, empowering energy to it. Having enough money to live comfortably and be free of financial worry is incredibly liberating. You will never catch me telling anyone to give up on money. I want you to find as many revenue streams as you can. I want you pulling in those Benjamins like they're coming out of a tissue box.

I recommend earning as much money as you need to do, have, and care for the things you love. But if you are pounding away at life doing shit that makes you miserable just because you think your own value is attached to an account balance, it's time to lighten the fuck up.

However, I took a long time to get level-headed and understand how passion and money must fuel each other. For many years, I was so obsessed with money as an "end," rather than as a "means to an end," that I was jacking with the energy of the whole financial institution and getting nowhere. All that time, I was stuck in this crazy, self-fulfilling prophecy called the scarcity mindset. What does the scarcity mindset mean? If you are convinced you will never have enough money…you won't. I know, that sounds nuts. You'd think that if you're worried about money, you'd work your ass off to make more. Nope – doesn't happen. You constantly sabotage yourself.

Want to see how that can happen? Let's time-travel back to 2005 when young Madison landed a job as an analyst at a Wall Street firm.

### Wall Street Blues

Oh lordy, how I loved the idea of Wall Street. So, when I got there in my analyst job, it was so exciting. My first day, this trader behind me got pissed off at something. He threw his fist through the screen, then slammed his phone down. He walked over to the sales area and got in a fistfight with some guy. Most of the folks in the room were so used to this shit that they didn't even look up. I was flashing back to all these cool movies that I'd seen: *Wall Street* and *The Boiler Room*, and I thought, "I hit the motherload! Look where I am now!" It was great! The bigshots were all high. Everything was so cutthroat, and shiny, and flashing by at the speed of light – the only thing missing was an eight-ball of cocaine on my desk and the DoubleMint Twins.

But it occurred to me, slowly, that nobody around me really seemed that happy. Over the next two years, I learned that only a small percentage of them actually were. Everyone else was an unpredictable, stressed-out maniac – both terrifying and hilarious.

They were all addicted to ridiculous gambles and dares. I remember somebody offering to pay $1,000 bucks to whoever could eat everything in the vending machine in eight hours. I said, "I can do that." And I did, though later I puked harder than I ever had before and I didn't shit for three days because I'd swallowed so much gum. But that's the stupid stuff you do to deal with being on edge all the time.

Because if you screwed up once, your job could just vanish. Or if somebody didn't like you. Or if you weren't dressed right. Speaking of dressing, it was important to me for people to take me seriously, so I went to Brooks Brothers and got myself the most unfuckable clothes ever designed and dressed like a dude for years, just to fit in. I stayed late with everyone else, putting in the "face time" because I never wanted to be the one who left at 5:30 p.m. when everyone else stayed until eight. I was terrified of taking a day off. It was a seriously stressful lifestyle. Somebody could just take it all away from you at any minute.

Oh yes, there was money, plenty of money. I wasn't even thirty years old yet, and living in a high-rise apartment in New York City, building the life I thought I'd always wanted.

But time passed, and we were heading straight into the 2008 financial crisis. You all remember this colossal screw-up? It was when all the big banks went tits up because they'd been financing bad mortgages - everyone and their dog was getting a mortgage, and it shouldn't have happened that way.

I began seeing situations around me where my coworkers might have been a bit over-leveraged. Might have thought that the cash flow money-train was going to keep rolling in forever, but it stopped, and it stopped *hard*.

Before I knew it, I was out of a job.

I had a stroke of luck here, though. In my apartment building, I often saw a gentleman who came home late at night, every time with a different girl. I finally asked him, "Are you the biggest player in New York?" That caught his attention. He laughed, and we started talking. He was starting up a new division of his Business to Business ("B2B") e-commerce company, and he asked, "Why don't you come over and run it?" So that's what I did. I jumped right in.

Now, in most professions, there's a term called "due diligence," and it means something a little different depending on, say, whether you're a lawyer, or an agent, or a broker, and so on. What it means is taking the time to do a comprehensive appraisal of the situation, so you can gauge the risk and the potential.

So as far as "due diligence" is concerned, I didn't really do, like, *any* of that, when it came to this career jump. I decided to live off my savings and work for sweat equity, which, looking back, was probably a mistake. For those of you who haven't had the pleasure, "sweat equity" is not a paycheck—it's investing your time and effort into a venture in the hopes that your contribution will pay off later. Sometimes, it works - and sometimes, there's a whole lot of "sweat" and no sign of any "equity."

Unfortunately, there were many different factors playing into our success, or lack of it, and we just didn't make it. We made mistakes (me included) and couldn't seem to grow, which put us all on edge. We also had different visions: I wanted to go into more commerce; they wanted to stay more B2B and focus on other things. Plus, we just didn't have the help we needed.

But that led me to a phone call with my father one night. I was agitated, frustrated, second-guessing myself, thinking, "What have I done? Did I screw my life up by leaving Wall Street?" I had let my Series 7 license expire, and you can't sell securities without one. Getting it back would mean taking that test again, and I didn't want to.

Dad said to me, "Madison, take the money out of it. If you could do anything you wanted to do in this world, and money wasn't a factor, what would you be doing?"

After a moment, I replied, "Well, I guess I'd be going around the world making people laugh."

"Sounds like you should be a stand-up comedian," said Dad.

"That is absolutely ridiculous," I said, and I continued with my life.

But from then on, every time I called Colorado to speak to my folks, Dad would ask me, "Did you go to an open mic night? Did you get on stage?"

Finally, in February of 2010, I took that leap of faith. I had put together a set, and I jumped on the stage at New York City's Eastville Comedy Club.

The rush of being onstage, pulling the audience into my experience and making them laugh was awesome and euphoric. If I could put that high in a pill and sell it, I'd be the richest drug dealer on the planet.

I thought to myself, *Oh yeah, this is it—I'm going to be a stand-up comedian. I will do this forever.*

Again though, I jumped into a career without doing any of that sweet, sweet due diligence. I was seduced by this combination of a "stage high" and knowing that comedians can make a shit-ton of money – 'cos I was always chasing the money.

Any comics – heck, any artist - reading this will laugh their asses off. Number one rule – you do not go into the "arts" to get rich. You go because you cannot help yourself, loving your art so much that eventually, someone else realizes you are fantastic and *then* the money comes. Few comedians really make it to what you'd call the "big time" where they're really getting rich from it, and you'd better believe they loved what they were doing, or they would never have made it so far.

So, here I was – living in a high-rise apartment in New York City, which I had snapped up when I thought I was going to be living on a Wall Street salary. In my opinion, I had "failed" at two different careers. Now, I was a struggling artist. The financial walls were caving in around me, and my paranoia and obsession about money became overwhelming.

### *Scarcity versus Abundance*

When you're living from paycheck to paycheck, you are in survival mode. Unintentionally, you might begin thinking in the *scarcity mindset.* A scarcity mindset is an obsession with what you lack, and usually, it applies to money or time. This toxic philosophy screws with your happiness and your thinking.

When I stepped into comedy, I was excited. I was going to follow my passion, not just a paycheck. I just had never expected how hard it would be, and how long it would take. I was so desperate for success (in the form of money) that it hadn't occurred to me that a career in stand-up comedy doesn't happen overnight. People work for years to make a living at it. That was when the scarcity mindset came on like a freight train.

When living with a scarcity mindset, the strange thing is, you believe that there will never be enough money, time, nor opportunity out there. Maybe it seems like that mindset should make you richer, because it amps you up to work harder and harder. But actually, the opposite is true. Scarcity mindset keeps you poor.

I began seeing my net worth as a sign of my value. I turned my desires into "needs." I needed to prove myself. I needed to be the wealthy one, I needed to be the one to grab the check at dinner.

Finally, I made the ultimate entrepreneur's sacrifice: I sold my 401(k) at the age of 30, taking the heavy penalty. I do not suggest doing that, ever ever ever! Get yourself a job as a stripper or a bartender or a senator before you sell that 401(k). You are cheating your future self, and your future self is going to be super pissed off at you!

Sure, I kept myself going. I thought, "I'm gonna make it. I'm gonna make it." But never for the right reasons. I worked to create proof for the world, but *not for myself.* I had to confirm to the world that I was good enough – because if you're rich, it means you're good enough, right?

Before I knew it, I absolutely could not afford that great high-rise apartment. Even though I had a roommate, I also had a bank account balance of close to zero. Friends, you can't walk outside your door in New York City without spending at least $25 bucks. Stand-up work isn't free either: I had to get myself out there, have headshots taken, and take cabs and subways to performances. When you're establishing yourself, many of the "sets" you do are for free. You're trying to get known and create a demand for yourself, and most importantly, hash out your material, which sometimes means giving it out for nothing. I started taking odd consulting jobs and doing temp work to make rent, and I felt embarrassed about having to resort to these stopgap measures.

I was one broke-ass bitch. But foolish pride kept me stubbornly struggling. I had declared myself a comic, and I was darn well gonna be a comic. A *rich* comic. I chased that money and kept telling myself, "I'm going to be somebody. I'm going to be validated one of these days." All the people who ever doubted me would feel so stupid, and I could tell them to get bent. I had "get bent" speeches practiced in my head. I wanted to be some big swingin' dick.

On the outside, I was saying, "I'm gonna be famous, tough, rich, and super-successful." But in my heart, I just wanted someone to tell me, "Hey, you can just relax. You don't need to work so hard. You don't have to prove anything to anyone. Nobody's going to dislike you or judge you."

I began to fantasize about being someone's well-protected housewife, putting myself in a situation where all my needs would be met, and I never had to make another decision.

I fretted, "Why can't I just suck the right dick? And never have to worry about this bullshit again. I'd be taken care of." I wanted a self-help book called *How to Suck the Right Dick* to show me the way. (True story: I considered using that title for this book, in fact, just because I thought it would make such a great gift. "Merry Christmas - I saw this book, and thought of you.")

Anyway, I lived on a scarcity rollercoaster for close to eight years. It never solved anything. I started believing that wealth would bring me problems – a bit of sour-grapes thinking that kept me from seeing clearly. "Even if I do get rich, everyone will be looking for a handout. I'll invest, and the stock market will crash. I'll buy property, and the real estate market will tank."

That was completely the wrong attitude, the wrong energy. It left me living in misery. Putting yourself into this scarcity mindset makes you panic, makes you prone to bad decisions, falling for "get rich quick" schemes, easy ways around doing real work that has real value. Even worse, your fear keeps you from seeing opportunity when it comes. You either don't respect the money you *do* earn, or you do nothing to earn more, and that keeps you absolutely broke.

Scarcity mindset keeps you suspicious of others, envious of their achievements, and certain that you are stuck. Envy is one of the most destructive emotions out there when it comes to making a success of yourself. We want so badly to have what other people have that we can lose sight of ourselves – forgetting that we might need something completely different in our lives.

### Making the Switch

So, here's how I finally managed to leave the scarcity mindset behind and start finding abundance in my life. I wish I could say I had some brilliant insight that opened the doorway for me, like a vision from my spirit animal, but really, the change was a matter of awareness. Suddenly, one day, I had "just enough" money that I didn't feel panicked any more. I got a little bit ahead. I was able to think clearly and see clearly for the first time in years.

In that moment of clarity, I thought, "This is how things need to be from now on. If I can have this security, this confidence, I can make things happen and keep moving forward." Money matters, and we need it. We need enough of it to free ourselves. We do that first, and the horizon rolls open. Here's how:

### Widen your income streams.

Do this, and you can stop living from paycheck to paycheck. You need enough money coming in that your bills are paid, and you don't have that pressure hanging over you.

### Work a little more.

Think of a time during the week when you just sit around on the couch doing nothing, and take that time to start a side-hustle. If you have time to watch Netflix, you have time to start a side hustle. There is so much you can do. You can make crafts to sell on Etsy, work freelance jobs through sites like Fiverr or Upwork, mow lawns, shovel snow, start a YouTube Channel, do affiliate marketing, sell pictures of your feet...yes people really do this. I am not recommending it specifically, but again, no judgement here, whatever it takes. As you can see, the possibilities are only limited by your imagination.

## Incorporate your side hustle.

The write-offs on your taxes alone are worth it; these perks come when you form a limited liability company (an LLC). LLCs are easy to research and form through your Secretary of State's website or through online legal services. Again, do your "due diligence" to see your best options.

## Stop expensive, useless habits.

Especially if they aren't bringing you joy! If you're paying through the nose for a car you can't afford just because you want to impress your friends, that's a problem. A lot of habits – smoking, drinking, dining out, lottery tickets, casino visits – are pretty expensive, and I would never tell you to stop doing something you loved, but maybe find a way to cut back. Deprivation isn't the answer, but moderation is. Once you see that money building up, it gets a whole lot easier.

*Invest.*

When you do have a little extra money, do not just stick it in the bank – nothing happens to it there. Invest in things that will pay you dividends. Invest at least 20 percent of your income, so that it is working for you. However you can do this – do it. It feels so good to have that money, you'll start wondering how to build up to 22 percent, and 25 percent, and on upward.

**Have a backup plan.**

In addition to your long-term investments, have an "emergency fund" of several thousand dollars (six to nine months of living expenses) in a high-yield savings account or investments that are easy to access. When unexpected expenses come up, you've got it. No need to panic. No need to crank up credit card debt.

*Summary*

Here's what's just crazy about this – switching yourself from a scarcity to abundance mindset is not much different from that old "glass half empty, glass half full" proverb. It's about attitude – leaving behind envy, defeatism, and hopelessness, and opening your mind to see opportunity, joy, and bounty.

But that doesn't mean it is an *easy* attitude adjustment. Moving your thinking from scarcity to abundance isn't something that happens overnight. It's a habit you must form by checking your thought processes daily, making certain that you're aligning your perceptions with the reality you want.

Here are some pointers to move from "scarcity" to "abundance" in your thinking. Like all paradigm shifts, this takes time and effort, so don't be discouraged if you don't have an overnight transformation.

- Express gratitude for what you have. In the middle of a scarcity mindset, it's easy to forget that you have a roof over your head, enough to eat, heat, electricity, and relative safety, and a lot of opportunities out there that you can take advantage of. Chances are pretty good that you've got a better life than many people in the world, so take a moment to count your blessings.

- Look for win/win scenarios that combine your passion with a solution. Passions don't always make you money, but solutions do. Passion carries you through the tougher times (see Chapter Two!).

- Hang out with people who believe in abundance.

- Teach yourself to recognize opportunity.

- Don't attach dollar figures to your projects. Work hard on what you want to work on, knowing it will bring money, and put your focus on your passion, rather than the payout. But again, make sure you are passionate about something that will make you money. We will discuss more further in the book.

And let me tell you something – there is so much money around the world. It constantly changes hands. What makes you think it isn't going to land in your hands?

However, sometimes, even after you establish an abundance mindset, those old interfering thoughts still try creeping back in. You'll think you've gotten lightyears beyond keeping up with the Joneses when suddenly, you'll find the scarcity mindset trying to take hold of your thinking. It's okay. We're only human. Beware of thoughts that sound like, "Everyone else's (fill in the blank) is better than mine," or "I'll never have enough money to (fill in the blank)," or "There's no room for me in the (fill in the blank)." Just acknowledge your feelings, recognize them for what they are, and move onward and upward.

Don't chase the money to prove something to someone else, or because you think your value is tied to your bank account. Don't "chase" money at all. *Make* money. Make the money you need to live the life you want, so you can have the ultimate goal one day…financial freedom.

Now shut this chapter and go make a list of things you can do to create passive income or areas you can cut back to save more and go kick some ass. We'll see you in the next chapter, so we can talk about whether "living your passion" is really going to pay the bills.

# CHAPTER TWO

## TIME TO FIND FINANCIAL FREEDOM

### Passions Versus Reality

One of my favorite quotes is from Oprah Winfrey, who said, "Follow your passion. Do what you love, and the money will follow."

First, Oprah is one to talk – her passions paid off in a honking big way, but we can't all be Oprah, either. And second, Oprah probably needed to be more specific because I know a few dudes whose passion is to jerk off all day long. Who knows? Maybe with OnlyFans, you *could* make money doing that today.

All jokes aside, you must be realistic. You gotta make rent, feed yourself, pay the electric bill, and more. You don't have to "get rich" to be happy – but if your goal is to get rich, make sure your passions align with that in mind. If your passion is to just have enough money to kick back and enjoy your family and your home, your passions can align with that, too.

I followed my passion when I stepped into stand-up comedy, and I don't regret that. My misstep was assuming that my passion would be enough for me to live on in the beginning, or in the middle, or maybe ever...I'm lucky that things worked out as well as they did, but I didn't know that back then, did I? You can't eat on hope. Dollars pay the rent, and not every passion brings in the dollars, especially not when you're first dipping your toes in the water.

Oh how I hustled those stages all over the country. When I worked, when the crowds were there and the jokes were hitting, I was high on performance, and I loved it.

But...when I didn't have bookings, when I was stuck at home, when I had time to think about my crappy bank account balance, when I wondered where the next money was coming from...that's when it hit me hard. So much for the "stage" high. I was absolutely miserable. There were nights I cried myself to sleep. I sometimes plummeted into real existential crisis, thinking things like, "Is life even worth living if it's going to be this hard?"

However I kept on hustling. I was lucky in that I had the encouragement of my family behind me.

Believe me, when I look back now at those times, I wish I'd let myself enjoy it more. Those were amazing experiences, priceless memories, and I spent a lot of my time fretting about the fact that I wasn't rich yet. When you're depressed and downhearted, try and remind yourself that in twenty years, your life is going to be a memory – what kind of memory do you want it to be?

Okay, so let's just face some facts. Chasing the money isn't the best way to live, but if you want to eat and keep a roof over your head, you do need it. Financial stress makes everything else harder. The world crashes in when you can't make ends meet. When you have a steady income, things are freer, more open, and creative. I always felt better when I had a consistent temp job, or I got good bookings for shows that actually paid me.

So, let's look at it this way…

## Free Your Finances/Free Your Mind

What does it mean to get "rich?" It's not the same for everyone; it's not even the same as wealth, really. "Rich" is measured in dollars, while "wealth" is measured by how much time you can "not work" without running out of money. I think what we all really want is financial freedom. My desire to get rich wasn't about buying Chanel bags to make my neighbors think I'm a better person. I think you'll notice, the wealthier someone is, the fewer "name brand" labels you'll find on their possessions.

They have nothing to prove by showing they can afford a $4,000 handbag. They can carry their shit in a paper sack and still move corporations around the world before breakfast time. So no, I won't buy myself the Chanel bag (*note to my future significant other, however: I would happily accept one as a gift*). Aim for the freedom to do what you want, when you want – then you'll stop buying the shit to impress people and focus on your own goals.

In the last chapter, I told you how I managed to finally climb over my scarcity mindset. Does it sound weird to say that getting more money is the answer to making more money? Yeah, it sounds like I'm some numb bitch who says, "You're poor? Why don't you try not being poor?"

Okay but look...it's true. If you ever want to get out of scraping, scratching, scrambling along, you've got to put yourself in a financially secure position and you do that by 1) increasing your income and 2) doing more with the money you have. The moment you free yourself from worrying about where next month's rent is coming from, you're able to dramatically expand your horizons and opportunities. Consider the early civilizations of the world for this example on a grand scale – groups of people who learned how to feed and shelter themselves through agriculture and architecture suddenly began to create art, science, medicine, culture – they blossomed because they didn't have to struggle to survive. You're not much different, plus you have indoor plumbing and air conditioning – that's a big win/win.

Don't ignore your passions or kick them to the curb, but look realistically at them. The kids who head for Broadway to be stars find a way to make ends meet – they wait tables or walk dogs or work as nannies – and we would never say they were "sacrificing their dreams." They gotta be able to get to that next audition fed and rested, so they gotta work.

I'm telling you, get to work. Don't let your pride stand in the way of making ends meet. I know it's not glamorous to be a waiter when you want to be a diva, but it's also not glamorous to dodge debt collectors or borrow money from your grandma. I had so many different jobs, from working as a front desk receptionist, to a consultant, and even an executive assistant, which was hard for me, considering I had a degree in finance, had worked on Wall Street, and even ran my own business. At times, it was a hard pill to swallow, but I had to do it to make my passion a reality.

### Gamify Your Life

When the financial markets choked in 2008, I wasn't as affected as much as other people because I wasn't making that much money, but the people who really were making some serious bucks had completely adapted to that lifestyle. They depended on it for their second or third homes or their children's private schools, and I got the feeling that a lot of them hadn't formulated anything like a "backup plan."

This abrupt switch in success-level hurt them badly. I watched them sell those homes, and even pull their kids out of private school. People who had been doing really well, some of the top traders, lost their jobs. It was rough to watch.

On the other hand, I had two friends from college who went into finance on the equity side of things, while I worked on the bond side. On their side of the fence, things were affected, but not quite as much; they seemed to not be as impacted by it. They still loved what they did, even though times were a bit more difficult.

And it clicked for me - these guys didn't go into finance for the money. They just genuinely loved finance, the game, the energy of it. Looking at them, I realized, "Holy shit - if you're not passionate about something, you won't have the drive or the excitement to make it through when times are rough." They saw finance as a game – and when was the last time you got stressed out and uptight over a game? I'm not talking about Uncle Brian, who flings the Monopoly board across the room rather than paying rent to his daughter (he is in the "scarcity" mindset, I'm afraid).

I also had another friend who was very successful, one of the most inspiring, fascinating people I've met. He really opened my eyes about something. You see, he had *lots* of money. I remember walking around his house and seeing money just scattered around. A $20 bill here, a $50 bill there, like bookmarks or sticky notes. Sometimes $100 bills. Or he'd pull something out of his pocket and some money would flutter to the floor.

I wondered, "How much money can he drop in a month without noticing?" So, I started picking it up. I went to him one day and said, "You've been dropping money. Here, I've collected it for you. You might want to keep a better eye on your cash."

"Oh thanks," he said, like it was no big deal. Well, it wasn't a big deal for him, because he was rolling in money. He told me, "Yeah, I already made *this* money. I'm more concerned about the *next* money I make." It was a game to him; he didn't do deals because of the money. He did them because he loved the game. His business was his passion.

We love games. We love to solve puzzles and strategize to find the best way to conquer, and even learn something so we can go back and do it better. We need to sit down to our work like we're logging into the greatest video game ever: the game of our life. You want to win, sure, but you also want to figure out the challenge and have fun with it. And if the challenge isn't going well, you can reset, strategize differently, try something new and even unexpected. If you can have fun with the challenges in your life, it makes an amazing difference.

### Financially Educate Yourself

Our schools don't teach us how to "do money," and that's a major problem. You may have your own theory as to why that is so – regardless, you're not going to find high schools telling kids about how to invest wisely, how to work smarter instead of working harder, the importance of having an emergency fund, what you need to do to qualify for loans or mortgages, good debt versus bad debt...I could go on for the rest of this chapter about what we're *not* taught to do, so let's just summarize by saying, "your educational system doesn't give a rat's ass if you're poor."

Some people learn financing from their parents (they're called "rich" people), and some learn it on their own when they realize that there's more going on than "work 40 hours a week, get a paycheck, pay taxes, hope for a raise." Our system is broken – I'm almost convinced it is purposely devoted to ensuring we stay poor or have just enough to get by. If you really look back at your education, it basically taught you to be a good employee, not become financially free so you could choose how to live your best life. It's almost as if someone "up high" convinced the system that there must be a poor working class for there to be a rich upper class – and volunteering *us* to be the former, rather than the latter.

Financial education is key because it means you know what to do with the money you have to keep it, grow it, and find opportunities with it to make more. It's the old saying, "Give two different people a million dollars each; one year later, one will just be broke again, while the other will have $2 million dollars, or more. The difference is financial education and, of course, mindset. The second person knew how to make that million work for them.

You don't have to have a ton of money to financially educate yourself. There's no excuse to not be financially educated. There are books, YouTube videos, and free classes everywhere that will tell you how to do more with the money you already have. You can also get a financial advisor to help educate you and keep you on track with your financial goals.

## Summary

Sometimes, a passion just needs to be a hobby or something you do in addition to bringing home the bacon. Sometimes, your passion can fuel your day job, or vice-versa. Sometimes, your passion can form a great added revenue stream, that extra money you need to put aside to stay out of debt and enjoy financial security and better yet, freedom. And sometimes, a passion can become your career and set you free.

In creating a balance between following your passions and making a living to live your best life, here is my recommendation. It's going to take a calculator and some deep thought, so be prepared.

1) Make a list of the things that you love (to have, to do, to create). Then, read them out loud to yourself and notice how you feel when you read each one. Which one or ones make you feel excited inside? That is typically a good way to really find out what your passion is.

2) Make a summary of the life you want to live (where, how much, how often, doing what, with whom).

3) Figure out how much that life will cost you.

4) Find out where your passions sit on that range of wants and costs, then consider what your passions can produce for you:

   a. Can your passions fuel your drive?

   b. Can your passions give you joy outside of earning money?

   c. Can your passions make added income?

   d. Can your passions fund your entire income?

You might find that your passions can make you very rich, or you might find that they should be more of a hobby. The point is, now that you are aware of your passions and what you need to make to live the life of your dreams, you can align your goals appropriately. Our passions make life worthwhile.

# CHAPTER THREE

## TIME TO STOP BEING AFRAID

I did stand-up comedy for twelve years and still do it from time to time. My focus these days is more on public speaking, for which stand-up comedy prepared me very well. But stand-up comedy is like that recurring naked-at-work nightmare, come to life in hi-def. There you are, alone, in front of a crowd that is expecting to laugh. You have a short amount of time to throw yourself on their mercy. You don't even have a soundtrack behind you to drown out the chirping of the crickets. And if you don't make them laugh, God knows what could happen. Hecklers. Anger. Tomatoes hurled at your head? Well, probably not...but then again...they might just feel sorry for you. Or even worse, they'll forget all about you. And now, the cold sweat starts to trickle down your spine.

In the middle of all that tension, I came up with the most terrible scenarios in my head. Not just that the audience wouldn't laugh, or that my act would bomb, but that the humiliation would mortally wound me so that I could never crack another joke. If I'd invited people to see me, they would think I wasn't any good, and they would distance themselves from me and pity me. Somehow, it would get back to everyone I ever respected: *Madison is a crappy comic, did you know? Better change your opinion of her.*

Of course, none of those things ever happened.

I was able to get out of that fear zone by visualizing success. If I didn't succeed, I visualized myself working on new jokes. If those new jokes didn't go over, I thought, *well thank goodness I had an audience to help me know what to fix.* Without a bad set every now and then, you never get any better.

Listen, I didn't get this fantastically wise overnight - it took some trial and error and tears and hysterical giggling. Nobody gets it right the first time around. I still have fears because you can't get rid of them - you just learn how to recognize them for what they are most of the time: just you, getting in your own way.

Now, I try to go through life believing everything's going to work out. And if it doesn't, well then, I just have faith. That speedbump was part of my story. I say, "Fuck the fear!"

### *How to Say "Fuck the Fear"*

Fear is a controlling factor in our lives, even if most of what we really fear is never going to happen.

You fear dating that new person because your heart might be broken again. Putting yourself out there is such a gamble, isn't it? Like, it's so much work just to get to know somebody and learn to trust and learn to relate. Then, suddenly, this person says, "Oh hey, I forgot to mention, I'm a king-sized asshole! Allow me to return your shattered dreams."

You fear moving to a new city because you might never make friends, find a good place to live, or find a great local beer or a stylist who won't cut your hair too short.

You fear any big decision because the devil you know is better than the devil you don't—you're not thrilled with your life now, but a big change might make your life a living hell. Better to stay put, never take that risk.

Look, life has no guarantees. Bad things can happen. None of us are promised another day on earth, much less happy outcomes 24/7. But a life lived in fear isn't much of a life, is it? Sure, there are real things that merit fear. Accidents. Crime. Sickness. Anal warts. But our fear of those things prompts us to wisely protect ourselves. We drive safely, buy insurance, get our prostate exams and PAP smears, use the buddy system, remember to look both ways before crossing the street. Fear doesn't have to control our lives.

Irrational fears are different animals. They stop us from moving forward. Remember when I talked to you about due diligence? Before we embark on any decision, most of us mentally weigh the pros and cons and then go ahead when the benefits outweigh the risks. Except when we buy lottery tickets.

But when fear gets the better of us, we stop seeing the "pros" and come up with more crazy "cons" than a hospital for the criminally insane. We might worry, "Moving to a new city means starting over, making new friends, finding new spots, maybe learning how to say 'y'all'..." Then, fear makes the crazy kick in. "What if I pick the wrong place to live and there's a murder hornet infestation? What if my parents fly to visit me, and Mom has a panic attack on the plane, and the NSA throws her in Guantanamo? What if there's a serial killer in the metro area who likes my type? What if everybody there listens to Genesis?"

From my experience, living *with* fear looks like living *without* faith. Fear means dreading what you can't see. Faith means believing in what you can't see. Live in faith and let go of that fear, and suddenly, you'll find yourself flying to freaking places that you never thought you could.

What's preventing you from starting that new business? Is it fear that things might not work out? That you won't be able to get the money? That you're going to blast through your savings? That your family and friends will think you're crazy? That someone else will do it better?

Your alternative is sitting at the same old miserable desk in your same old miserable job and thinking, *I wish I wasn't scared. I wish I would have tried that.*

The greatest entrepreneurs in the world experience fear. The difference is, they never let it stop them. You know that Jeff Bezos or Elon Musk or Richard Branson had moments when they wondered, "Am I doing the right thing? What if this all goes wrong?" But they move past fear and right into action to try things, and they know that even when failures occur, it is all part of the process. Their refusal to let themselves be stopped by any constraints is what sets them apart.

Everybody feels fear. It's a natural emotion. Don't run from it or excuse it. Acknowledge it. "Okay, I'm afraid. Why?"

If fear is truly getting in your way, I highly recommend that you journal and write it all down. If you don't like writing, talk to a trusted friend. Sometimes, the act of writing something down, or saying something out loud, takes a lot of the "scary" out of it.

Ask yourself these questions: "What am I really afraid of? What would I do if that fear really came true? What would my life look like?"

You might discover some surprising things about "what you fear." Like, that your fear is highly unlikely—hey, I think about 99 percent of the shit we worry about never comes true. Or that an outcome isn't so scary after all. Or that it is a contingency you will be able to handle. Or that it's actually a doorway to tremendous success and joy.

Let's spell this out. You're afraid to go on that date because your heart has been broken before. Write it down. "I'm scared that if I go on this date, we'll hit it off, and start dating more seriously. Pretty soon, I'll fall in love. I'll be planning a wedding while my significant other is stealing my savings to pay for fetish porn. And it'll end like all my relationships end. Me, with a busted heart."

Now look at this with some logic. First, there is no point in looking at a "date" like there are only two possible outcomes: either you have one lousy night, or you end up two years down the road with another demolished relationship and another broken heart. Although, I will say, if you go on your date with that kind of attitude, outcome number one is pretty likely.

But there are so many other things that might happen. Isn't it better to come toward a new experience with faith that things will work out well? When we come into our days and experiences with the attitude, "I have a good feeling about this," that actually turns out to be true much of the time. Because, pardon me for sounding like a real Pollyanna here, but nothing makes for as many positive outcomes as a positive outlook.

Let's wind back to that great fear: your re-broken heart. All right, let's say that does happen. You invest yourself in a new relationship and it goes tits-up. Is that entirely a bad thing? Didn't some good come out of it? You got one step closer to the person you're supposed to be with. You learned more about what you want and what you don't want.

Remember two things as you're fearing that rejection (or any other fear that is sinking its claws into your brave heart):

1) You survived; and

2) They may no longer feel like failure, hurt, or mistakes.

Think about those times when you thought your life, or at least a significant part of your life, was simply *over*. For a while there, you felt like the chorus of every country/western song written in the 1970s. Mighty sad, Tex. But, was it really *over*? Were you truly damaged beyond all repair? You'll find as the years go by that a lot of failures, hurts, and mistakes can start feeling like course corrections, important lessons, and, as the saying goes, "dodging a bullet."

Every time you're fearful, say, "You know what? I have faith that the Universe (or God, or fate, or karma, or my own badass bitchness) is going to protect me. I'm going to take those chances. And if it doesn't work out, well, maybe it's guiding me on the path where I need to be."

A life without chances is a boring, boring life. Take those chances. Go meet the new people. Go do something you've always wanted to do. Go do something that makes the folks at your family reunion say, "You're crazy!" Yeah, right – and they're still listening to country/western songs from the 70s.

It is amazing how often we end up exactly where we are supposed to be.

### Who Cares What They Think?

One of our biggest fears in the world—and the one that we need to kick to the curb the fastest—is this: "What will people think?"

For a good long time while doing comedy, I cared too much what people thought, preventing me from really taking the risks I needed to on stage. There is nothing that will kill a comedian's career faster than worrying about the opinions of others. Once I learned to accept that we cannot possibly please everyone, and screw them all anyway if they're gonna be like that, I was able to make better career decisions to move me forward into an abundance of opportunities.

You cannot, cannot, cannot get anywhere valuable worrying what other people think. Oh, you can get somewhere, sure enough. Somewhere you don't like, somewhere that feels like a lie, somewhere where you're surrounded by assholes who only care about how you look or how much money you have. You can get up to your eyeballs in debt. You can get twenty years down the road in a relationship or a career that you never really wanted. There is a lot of shit you can do when you care what other people think—but it is just that: a lot of shit.

Realize not everybody is going to like you, okay? No matter how good of a person you are, no matter how nice you are, how great you are, how rich, thin, pretty, buff, or successful. Doesn't matter. Someone's not going to like you for some reason that's probably outside of your control. So, let go of the opinions of others.

Obviously, when you go into a job interview or a pitch meeting, you do worry about what they think because you want them to say yes. That's okay. That's a healthy opinion. When you meet your future in-laws, you probably don't want them thinking their offspring would be better off marrying into the Manson family.

I can't sit here and tell you that I never think about what people think at all. No. There are still times when I do. But I just prepare myself by thinking, "Okay, *why* am I worried about what they think?" I try to piece together whether I believe this is a person who can have some influence over my life. Is this a person I want to emulate, or ingratiate myself to? And what you discover may be some crazy competitive nonsense that has slipped into your mind saying, "You need to be golden in so-and-so's opinion," when in reality, they don't really matter, and you shouldn't really care.

Should we post that picture on social media? Should we go after that business? Should we date that person? Should we wear that sweater, or drink that beer, or admit that we loved the movie version of *Cats*? *I don't know what people are going to think of me. What if they think that I'm less? What if they think that I should have done more? Done something different? Done a better job?*

I've got two things to say about that kind of thinking:

First, who gives a crap what they think.

Second, whatever they're thinking, it's probably not about

you.

Yeah, the truth is, we're all pretty self-involved. We're obsessed with our own lives to the extent that we very seldom pay any lasting attention to what other people are doing. I have a friend that doesn't want to go to the pool because she's over 55 and self-conscious about how she looks in her swimsuit. Swimming would be really good for her, but she refuses to let herself reap the benefits because she's so worried about her appearance that she can't enjoy herself. I tell her, "Nobody cares how you look. They're all worried about how *they* look." Her fear of others' opinions keeps her from doing something that would help her, something that she would probably really enjoy.

Point is, if it makes you happy, and makes your heart sing, and you're not hurting anyone, then that's what you need to do. That's what is going to make you thrive, and that is what life is all about: thriving and taking the chances. Even "failure" means you took a chance – people who never fail, never take chances, and I promise you at the end of their lives, they'll wish they'd risked more and failed more and tried more. Don't be that person.

## Summary

There are some things in the world that are legit scary. And there are things you should do to protect yourself from them.

For example:

Psycho killers – scary! Lock your doors. Learn judo. Distance yourself from people who look way too interested in wearing your skin.

Bears – dangerous! They look adorable, but they're cranky as hell. Don't mess with bears. Leave them to their salmon and honey.

Wasps – awful! Like, they're the worst. I mean, they're cranky like bears and scary like psycho killers.

And other things: war, death, disease, famine – Biblical shit that haunts us. No guarantees, either. But still, come on. Buy some good insurance. Get your annual physical. Check your blind spots. Look before you leap. Most of the time, there are practical, simple things we can do to improve our chances in the world. And if there aren't, then everyone runs the same risk, and that's just part of life. It may even be kind of exciting – and sometimes scary shit is needed to make things change, happen, and improve the world.

But how awfully sad to spend your time living in terror of the most pointless, impotent threats of all: the fear of failure, the fear of disappointment, the fear of embarrassment, the fear of other people's opinions. If this is the kind of stuff holding you back, take the first steps to lightening the fuck up by examining these feelings. Write it down, talk it out, find out what is *really* scaring you.

Ask yourself if fifty years from now, you want to admit that *this* was the fear that held you back.

I bet the answer is, "No. Never!" Fuck the fear.

# CHAPTER FOUR

## TIME TO STEP INTO FAITH

### *Believing in Things You Can't See*

Writing a chapter about God in a book that uses the f-word in the title feels a little weird…but I'm gonna do it. I believe our God is such a loving, humorous God, that He would never hold it against me.

Where religion turns a lot of people off is when it turns God into a humorless "do this, don't do that" set of rules - and I just don't know how much God really had to do with that. He made us with senses of humor and a love for funny, naughty words. I see God as loving us in all our flaws, wanting us to live our best lives, and pleased when we learn our amazing lessons. We're the ones who place judgments on ourselves and other people.

Gotta tell you though, this chapter is going to have at least 50 percent fewer dick jokes than the others. I just feel like a certain amount of respect is due…like, "Tone it down for a minute, Madison, we're trying to talk about God here." But don't worry. I promise that the dick jokes will soon return, and that God will be fine with it.

Some of the most influential, successful people in the world thank God first for what they have, and there is a reason for that. He is the Creator. I'm saddened by the idea that faith has become controversial. People aren't as vocal about their beliefs anymore because faith in God has fallen out of fashion. That may be because we confuse organized religion with God. They're not the same thing.

I grew up in a Christian household. I was raised to know God and love God. My parents never forced religion down my throat, but I was expected to go to church and understand what it meant. When I got to high school, my parents let me make the choice of whether I would continue practicing faith, knowing I needed to think for myself.

And as you might predict, when they stopped making me go to church, I stopped going. I had teenage things to do. But my parents kept going to church and even Bible study on Friday nights, which meant that I didn't have to lose my virginity in the back of a car.

But along with not attending church, I even stopped praying. I remember telling other people, "I'm not religious. I'm spiritual." At the time, I saw religion as manmade and divisive. Wars are fought over religion. People argue bitterly over their beliefs; it divides families and ends friendships. I didn't like the idea of anything that separated people. I didn't like anything that excluded certain people, implying to them, "If you're not part of this religion, you can't come in here. You can't be a part of this. You can't enjoy these things."

What I've found since then is that when you put your trust and faith in a Divine Being, a Creator, and a Protector, and don't adhere yourself rigidly to an organized system of thought, it is easier to find commonality with others. Whatever faith means for you, I encourage you to embrace, cherish and love it.

My belief is that God created all of us. *We* created religion. He loves us, no matter what you choose to practice for your faith - or not.

But just like anyone, God's help doesn't come if He doesn't think you need it. So, you must ask.

## *The Power of Prayer*

I remember going through constant turmoil while I was struggling to succeed in New York. I felt increasingly depressed and anxious. I spoke to my Mom and Dad at least every Sunday night. I asked them a lot, "Please pray for me. Have your group pray for me. Pray for my success, that I won't feel sad, that I'll find my path, even that I'll just get the apartment I want."

And they would. I'd run into family friends on my trips home, and they often said, "We've been praying hard for you!"

After many years of this, my mother finally said to me, "Madison, we will always pray for you. But do you pray for yourself?"

I didn't. I had to say, "No, I don't pray for myself. How do you even do that?"

"Just talk to God like you are speaking to a friend," she explained. "Have a conversation. Ask Him for help with things you can't do on your own."

"Sure, I'll think about that…" I said, but I didn't do it. More time passed before her message really began to get through to me. I read other people's books. I tried other people's methods. But eventually I had to admit that, whatever I was doing, it wasn't working. Maybe by handing my concerns over to God, I could at least get some clarity, feel some peace. So, I thought I'd give it a try.

I got my chance when a problem came along that I couldn't solve by myself. I was busting my ass to get a big contract signed for a show I was working on. We had trouble: the person who needed to sign was trying to cut me out of the deal, giving me a really hard time. I never saw it coming down the pipeline. I felt so sad and insulted, plus my anxiety was building—and there was nothing I could do to change things. Attorneys were involved at this point. Mentally and emotionally, I felt exhausted.

But that night, I closed my eyes and said, "God, I really want this to happen. I know that you can make this happen. I can't do it on my own, so I'm giving it up to you. If this is in my best interest, I know that you will make this happen for me."

I was actually able to sleep that night. I woke up the next morning, refreshed and relaxed, enjoyed a shower, got myself together, and hit the coffee shop. Only then did I check my email… and there it was. The contract was signed. I remember thinking, 'Wow. *Wow*. Thanks, God! This guy is good!" It became a story I shared with friends. "You know, the coolest thing happened the other day…" But there was nothing else I needed, and some time passed before I had another conversation with God.

Then a day came when I really wanted a certain someone cast for a show I was working on. My agent called and said, "I'm talking to this guy in five minutes, and I'll have an answer for you." I said, "Great!" I hung up and turned to God, remembering how right it had felt the last time I handed a problem to Him.

"God, I really want this person on my show. It'll change my life, and his, and it will change the people who get to see it. He's the perfect person. If it is meant to be, let it be, and if not, I trust that you'll show me the way to get it done."

Ten minutes later, I got a text saying he was in. The contract was signed.

"This Guy works so fast!" I exclaimed – meaning God, not my agent – no offense to my agent.

Prayer is, in my definition, reaching out to God, to put events into His hands. Now listen - I wholly believe in God in the Christian sense. You may not believe in God, or your concept of God may be different from mine. I'm not trying to convert you, only to suggest that being in communication with a power greater than yourself, no matter what you decide to call it, can be an immeasurable boon.

When I talk about my faith, I'm not pushing to make it your faith. I just want you to find faith in something. And I want you to pray.

For me, prayer isn't just "talking to God." It is also creating a positive, optimistic, and reflective energy, that you are going to get what you want because you are ready to receive it. That is the Law of Attraction. In a nutshell, it's like ordering out of a catalog: pick what you want, nothing is too big or small. You simply must believe, and now, that it is your reality. That's what prayer is. Trusting in something you can't see.

When I wanted to write this book, I didn't know how I would do it. I kept writing down ideas and summaries, and thinking about how great it would be. Still, I was stalled out. But you can't just wait around for things to happen – that means a whole lot of waiting and not a lot of happening.

So, I prayed about it. "God, please show me the way. I'd like to write a book. I want to go on a speaking tour to help and encourage more people in person. I want to bring in my comedy. I want to get back on stage. I want to keep doing what I love."

A week after I said that prayer, I ended up at a Mastermind meeting in Mexico where I met my publisher.

Put faith and reflective prayer at the center of your life; and you'll watch things change immediately.

## Drop the Ego and Embrace Faith

Ego is something that I believe truly gets in everyone's way. Ego is the opposite of faith in God. Faith is a true inner voice that says, "I'm going to trust in something I can't see, but I know it's going to work out, and I know my Creator is going to guide me through."

Ego is what happens when you're not feeling good about yourself. We all have those experiences when we know our ego is running the show.

Like this. Sometimes you run into somebody you haven't seen in a bit, someone you want to think well of you, and they ask, "How's it going?" At that moment, maybe you're not feeling great about your career or your relationships—you just really don't want to talk about it. The ego snaps into play because you don't want to look like a loser—a perception that started in your own head—and you become all about defensiveness and negativity. And lies. Lies come in there, too. You say, "Everything's *great*. I have this, and this, and this, like, I'm so fulfilled I could just explode."

Ego is what tells you that you need a nicer car than your neighbor, a bigger house than your friend Bob, and nicer clothes than Chad and Stacy.

Need? No. You don't. You only need what's best for you.

If you're buying shit to impress other people, your priorities are wrong. Do you want that nice car and that big-ass house because you love them and they will be a productive part of your life? Yes? Then that's awesome, that's exactly what I want for you. But if you're plunging toward that nice car and big-ass house just to stroke your little ego, then you're doing it for the wrong reasons - and you probably don't have the money to afford it because if you *did* have the money to afford it, your ego probably wouldn't be so big.

You may have noticed multimillionaires and billionaires dress in really simple, no-name-brand clothes, live wherever they want, play five-dollar minimums on the blackjack table - they don't care. Ego is not in the forefront of their minds; instead, they are driven by passion. The ego makes you insecure, saying, "You're not good enough." The ego turns you into an asshole. Don't be that person - you don't need to prove anything to anyone.

Drop the ego, or at least check it at the door, and all your relationships will get better. Even your meetings will get better and people will certainly say nicer things behind your back. "Wow, I can't believe how cool that person is." You won't get that kind of feedback if your ego leads the way into the room. It just rears its big jackass head when you're not happy with something going on in your life. It pops up like a defensive shield of armor, to protect you, so you'll still "look good." Too bad human beings are excellent at spotting when someone doesn't have the goods to back up the bluster.

I had this happen in my career. I kept working so hard, and I had nothing to show for it yet...but everything was moving, and things were going great. I couldn't wait until that next moment when I could announce something, but I couldn't just yet. So, ego came into play. Other artists or comics asked me, "Well, how's it going?" So, I said, "Everything's great. Couldn't be better. I've got all this cool stuff in the works, and life is so good!" But that tone was ego talking. I had to take a step back and be honest. "It's taking a little longer than I expected, but I'm so happy that I followed my passion. I really hope you'll be able to see something soon!"

Ego is what makes you want things from people. When you walk away from someone because "they can't do anything for me," that's your ego at work. When you're looking for someone prettier or richer, more famous, more important, than the person you're speaking to at an event, that's your ego trying to make you believe in your own importance. I've had that happen at events, when I'm speaking to someone and catch them looking over my shoulder, trying to find someone more important to speak with. I lost respect for that person, but it also made me feel really shitty. That was their ego at play – and then mine, too.

When you go with God, and let go of the ego, you'll feel cleaner. Better about things. Your situation will brighten because you'll be able to appreciate what you have instead of regretting what you don't. And life is simply too short for regrets. Have faith that your higher power has and will continue to bring you the things that are in your best interest.

## Summary

If you're struggling with something, like a broken heart, failed relationships, your career, money, a dream that you want to come true, don't stress because you have somebody upstairs rooting for you, who is always going to guide you in the right direction. Just remember that. When you want something big, pray for it. You don't have to get down on your knees—God hears you anywhere, anyhow. Next time you want a little push, a little faith, a knowledge that there is something of love so immense you cannot imagine it cheerleading for you, it's there, waiting for you. Tap into it.

When life seems not to be going your way, when last-minute changes happen, when the unexpected flies in your face, keep this in mind. There is a plan. There is someone watching out for you. Your life and the events it contains happens for your benefit. Your higher power has a way of putting you exactly in the right place. Always keep in the forefront of your mind that your life is set out for *you*.

Finally, remember – life's tests are sometimes hardest right before the breakthrough. It is up to you to keep your faith – it's okay to cry, it's okay to doubt, and it's okay to disagree. Faith is strong enough to withstand all of it. God will see you through the path that is best for you.

# CHAPTER FIVE

## TIME TO CREATE YOUR NEW AMAZING REALITY

**Perception Perfection**

Perception is such a basic tenet of experience that all self-help books seem to bring it up, and the concept is basic.

*How you choose to perceive your life is how you will experience it.*

Two people see the same painting, movie, advertisement, sunrise, event, party, sexual partner...Geez, just fill in the blank...and interpret it differently because they're coming at it with different brains built from two different lives, duh. But the kickass thing about perception is that it's malleable, flexible—it's the modeling clay of experience.

If your perceptions are skewed, you'll create obstacles for yourself. Changing your perception is one of the easiest, quickest ways you can start knocking those obstacles out of your way.

And you don't even have to trick yourself. This is one of those methods that is obvious and available to anyone who is willing to do it. Sure, it takes a little practice, but once you've gotten into the habit of spinning your experiences toward the positive end of the dial, you'll feel the benefits fast, and you'll want to keep on doing it.

Maybe there's someone you're interested in romantically. They don't call you back. You choose to see it as personal rejection. "Something is wrong with me," you think. "I'm too fat, skinny, plain, boring, stupid, poor…" or whatever the thing you're beating yourself up about today. Or you don't get a job. "Oh shit, I'm so stupid and nervous and my résumé sucks, and I always screw up interviews."

Can you perceive this differently? Like, "Never mind, it just wasn't a good fit for me. Now the path is clear to get what is right for me."

I've heard this from countless successful actors (who are good-looking) and businesspeople (who are brilliant and savvy) - yes, they get rejected too. They tell me, "I don't worry about what I don't get, because then I know, it's not for me. Whatever *is* meant for me, I'm going to get." They're not discouraged when someone beats them out of a role, a deal, or a position. They keep a positive perspective on their experiences.

Which is not to say it doesn't take some practice. I used to go through life with a perception of self-pity, thinking critically about myself and taking everything personally. Rejection sucks, because so much of the time, we don't know the reasons for it. All we know is that we were rejected, and our logic tells us, "It had to be me," because we have no idea what else was happening, so it becomes personal and demoralizing. But until you can get into the head, life, and experiences of the person who rejected you, you can't actually know anything. We don't have time to list all the reasons why rejection might come your way. You cannot take the blame completely onto yourself when there are infinite other possible reasons why you weren't a good fit.

Think back to a time when you rejected someone or something—a romance, a job, an opportunity. Did it have something to do precisely with the person involved? Probably not; it was more likely about where you were in your life, what you needed, and what was best for you at that point.

Rejection is no longer personal for me because I've learned to view it as a force that moves me closer to my end goals. Pretty recently, there was this opportunity I truly wanted to take advantage of. I would have learned a lot from it. I believe in learning everything I can; more knowledge means more value means more money, y'know?

Then, rejection came down.

I kind of held my breath, waiting to feel bummed out. Younger Madison would have panicked, thinking, "Oh what's wrong with me, how come I can't get this deal done, I'm so stressed, blah blah blah…" But it never happened. I actually felt excited. I thought, "You know what? God's got my back; He's keeping me on the path. I didn't get this for a reason. Something bigger is coming down the pipeline, and this particular deal would have distracted me from reaching that goal."

It's not always easy to find things bright or cheerful in our world. We're surrounded by a lot of negative stuff. Sit and scroll hours of social media or binge the news for an hour, you'll probably start feeling extremely depressed. That shit, you cannot control. So, say, "Fine – I can't control the news, but I do have the control to turn this crap off and go outside and enjoy some beautiful nature." Or play with your pets, or get busy with your bae, or papier-mâché yourself a pinata. Whatever makes you smile, that's the point. The world hasn't necessarily changed. All that bad shit may still be going on, but you can't control it or even influence it, so why stew in it? When you focus on what is positive and good around you, not only are you feeding that energy back to the rest of the world, but suddenly, you've lightened the fuck up!

Honestly, in the great game of life, there's not a whole lot you *can* control. You certainly can't control other people, nor events that occur suddenly and unexpectedly. Use your perception to help yourself see the lesson, the humor, the opportunity, the redirection.

## Visualization and Manifestation

I believe in vision boards. I don't believe in crafting though – no thanks scissors and glue! I guess in the pioneer days when they made vision boards, they had to carve shit out of trees or weave it from corn and nail it all together, and then before computers, people had to cut things out of magazines and glue it to paper, like they were putting together ransom notes. Now, we have tech that keeps us out of the school supplies aisle.

I've interviewed so many self-help coaches on my podcast, and they would always talk about the importance of creating vision boards. Then, I'd speak with successful businesspeople, and they'd mention their vision boards. They would talk about other things, but vision boards always seemed to come up.

I'd done one of those posterboard vision boards years ago, and now, it was time for an update. I built my most recent vision board into a PowerPoint, so I can scroll through the images on my computer, then upload it. This way I can update it easily any time.

When I did this new vision board, I looked it over and thought, "Oh my, the shit on this vision board is probably worth

200 million dollars." Ten years ago, I would have thought, "I'm not living on the same planet as everyone else—this ain't reality."

But having these things no longer sounds crazy to me. In fact, there were more things I could have added because I'm stepping into all this opportunity that I have prepared and worked for - none of it feels out of reach any more.

You are the only one limiting you from getting what you want, because you don't believe it's really yours. A vision board lets you visualize your desires to believe they are possible.

I usually look at my vision board before I have a big meeting I'm jazzed about. I spend five minutes before the meeting staring at my vision board, to get myself excited about what's coming. I look at my future home, my future vacation home, my future family, my future awards, and I think, "Yes, this is my life. I am ready to step into this opportunity." Every time I look at this vision board, I get this massive dose of positivity, because I know I'm getting closer to obtaining these things.

This leads us into manifestation. You know by now that I believe in the power of God. I can't see Him, but I have faith that He is there. This is how you must be with the things you want from your life. You may not be able to see the $1 million, or the $10 million, or the $100 million in the bank account. But you must believe that it's going to get there – and suddenly, the

Universe says, "Huh, looks like they're ready for success!" And here come your opportunities.

It took me so many years to drill this idea of visulalization/ manifestation into my head, because I had all these other blocks in my life, not to mention the fact that I was stubborn.

The following exercise is one that I learned to practice. Yours won't be exactly the same, but I hope you'll get the idea.

First, put on some beautiful music – something that inspires you. Then, quiet your mind and picture your dream life playing out like a movie. Picture yourself perhaps ten years in the future. You can also voice record yourself over soft music, so you can play it back as it walks you through your manifestation. An example of a voice recording you could do, would be:

*'You just found out you have the money to buy your dream home. You are in the car with the realtor, and they are driving you to visit some homes. What does the car look like, feel like, smell like? What are you wearing? How do you feel?*

*You pull up to the home. What does it look like, where is it located? You walk into the house. How does it smell? How is it laid out? Walk yourself through this home, taking your time exploring each room.*

*Now, walk to the backyard. What does it look like? Really concentrate on all the detail. Now, walk into the kitchen. The relator tells you how much the house is. You smile, knowing you can afford to pay cash.*

*You pull out your checkbook and write the check. Notice how you feel, knowing that the house is all yours.*

You can also do this with anything you want to manifest, whether it is a new job, the perfect partner, a dream vacation… Really have fun with this.

This is an important aspect: in order to manifest, keep your visualization in present tense. Don't say "I wish, I want, I hope." Keep it in the "right now," like this:

- I am making a difference in people's lives.

- I am married to my best friend.

- I am innovating in my field.

- I am making X dollars a year.

- I am traveling everywhere I want to go.

- I am happy with my life.

Believe these things like they are already true, and you'll walk around with your shoulders straight and your head held high. You are confident, but not cocky. You know who you are, and that things are happening for you. When people meet you, they will know it, too.

I know, it seems weird to run around saying to yourself "I am rich," when your bank account might not reflect that yet, but you must believe before you can receive! The first time I tried to grasp this concept, I kept thinking *I better not say these things out loud or someone is going to throw my ass into a mental institution.* When I first learned about the Law of Attraction, I thought, *What the fuck? I'm supposed to walk around like I can afford all this shit?* Well, yeah – but keep it to yourself, so people don't think you're nuts. And don't use it as an excuse to make dumb decisions – until you *really* have the money, don't buy the Ferrari. It's about living with the mindset that your Ferrari – or whatever – is within your reach, so that you can easily see, access, and receive all the ways to get it.

No one needs to know your visualizations but you. Trust me, it works!

Another tool I like to use to manifest/visualize is right before bed. Everyone has a little brainstorm when they lay their head down at night, so next time you're getting ready to drift off to sleep, visualize and elevate yourself in your mind. See yourself in that home, that job, that relationship. Believe that it is possible for you.

Visualize yourself meeting the person you would love to work with – be it Stephen Spielberg or Elon Musk or Paul McCartney or Warren Buffet. Really imagine the encounter. How would you act? Be realistic—would your palms be sweaty, would you feel nervous, trip over your words, jiggle your knees? And if so, what could you do to change that? And imagine yourself changing it. Imagine the nerves and the intimidation fading away. Picture what you want from this person—mentorship, partnership, or maybe just a pic for your Instagram. Visualize building a rapport, making a great pitch, shaking hands, and having a laugh together, until you see it all working perfectly. You are in effect telling the Universe that you are ready to meet this person.

### Why Don't You Meditate?

When people suggest I meditate, I just want to tell them to back off.

Okay, yeah, that's a little harsh. It's nothing personal. If you can quiet your mind for half an hour and focus on nothingness, great for you. I can't. It's hard, it's boring, and it just doesn't seem to work for me.

That does not mean, however, that I don't know the benefit of calming and centering myself. Everyone should figure out their own best method for grounding themselves in the "now" and calming their mind, so they can keep their head literally and figuratively.

I just must do it in a quick-and-easy way. What has worked for me and might for you as well, is breathing in slowly for eight seconds, really focusing on my breath. I then hold it for another eight seconds and then breathe out for eight seconds. I do this as many times as I need to feel calm and centered.

Another thing that is important and one of the key benefits of meditating is being able to become more responsive than reactive. When something bothers you, hurts you, enrages you, take a deep breath and pause. This will allow you to be more responsive, instead of just reacting in a way that you might regret.

This is a fantastic way to tell your central nervous system that you're not in danger, so all those panicking hormones rushing to your defense can check themselves. You can reset your thoughts. Face it—while you're holding your breath, you're probably not thinking about much else. And yes, seconds do matter. A few seconds can keep you from saying something stupid, from hurting someone's feelings, from making an ass of yourself—it can give you time to think, time to come up with a response, time to make a plan of action. Taking a long, deep breath is the on-the-spot equivalent of "Wait until morning to send that angry email," because you *never* want to send that angry email until you've had a chance to think it over.

If you, like me, have trouble with meditation, allow me to suggest the following relaxation regimen:

### Madison's "Toilet Time" Relaxation Exercise

People discount toilet time when it's actually a valuable part of your life. You're ridding your body of toxins and performing a satisfying biological act that almost always makes you feel better. So, while you're already there, doing good things for yourself, *take that time to do a whole body/mind reset*!

1) Start with some deep breathing exercises. What!? It's not like anyone's going to bother you.

2) Think about things you're grateful for. "Oh look! Plenty of toilet paper!"

3) If there's not a line waiting outside the door, you can even get in a quick twenty squats. I'm telling you, do twenty squats every time you pee, and you'll have one fine ass.

There are only two rules.

- Never do squats or deep breathing or gratitude exercises while there is a line for the bathroom. That's not cool.

- Don't take your phone to the bathroom. That is so *nasty*.

## Summary

Your thoughts create your choices and your reality. Where you're at in life, in this exact moment, is all a result of those. Everything you've done in your life has led to this moment.

If this moment is not a happy one for you, you are justified to ask yourself, "What was I thinking? What led me to this?" Then, identify the path if you can – it is different for everyone, and it may stretch back many, many years. As soon as you find yourself pinning the blame on someone or something else, change your perception. You cannot alter what happened in the past, but you can alter the way you perceive it. "I am unhappy because I had a heartbreak," you might say. That's rough, but it's not exactly true. Think about it. The truth is probably more like, "Maybe I am unhappy because I haven't learned to find the value in my heartbreak."

Heartbreak sucks. But adversity can make you strong, resilient, innovative, compassionate, and empathetic. Could we be those things without getting our hearts smashed to pieces? Sure, and it would be nice. Life is going to serve you some sucky breaks, though – finding a way to perceive them more positively makes them hurt less, and heal faster, and appreciate the people and experiences without being tainted by pain and resentment.

Finally, you don't have to meditate – but find something in your life that lets you relax and reset. If "Madison's Toilet Time" Relaxation Exercise does it for you, great!

I'm writing this to wake you up. Your thoughts and choices create your reality. If you don't like your reality, you are the *only* one who can do anything to change it. Don't wait around for magic. Make your own.

# CHAPTER SIX

## TIME TO BELIEVE IN YOURSELF

### *Don't Wait for Them: Validate Yourself*

We are brainwashed by our upbringing and society to believe that validation needs to come from outside. We're trained to feel good about ourselves when we get compliments, trophies, awards, and accolades. Make your parents and teachers proud, be a good team player, do what it takes to make everyone like you.

We're not often taught the importance of finding inner validation.

I see two layers of this - the first is more superficial, and it's something we shouldn't do to ourselves. We look for extra validation wherever we can get it. We ask, "Do I look nice?" when we know already that we look nice; we say, "Oh gosh I look so fat, so old, so terrible..." waiting for our friend to say, "No, you look *fantastic*, I wish I looked as good as you!" because luckily, most people will lie for you. Not too many assholes out there who will respond, "You know - you *are* looking really old. I have a great Botox gal; do you want her number?"

The second, deeper level of validation that you can achieve, is more about having faith in your abilities and your value as a magnificent human being. I'm amazing at what I do. I love it when I get to show the world the things I've done. I have something to offer. I am worthy of the things I want, and the things I achieve. I am more than the sum of my money and possessions. I am the creation of a divine and loving force.

I used to judge myself based on my bank balance. That was actually a source of confidence for me. When it was low, I thought, "I'm not good enough (*for whatever*) because my bank balance is pathetic." I saw myself as a struggling artist, so that's exactly what I was. And I was looking good, people told me, "You're pretty, you look great!" but on the inside, I was a mess. I'd hold myself back from a relationship with someone who was interested in me, because I wasn't rich yet and thought I didn't have much to offer.

So, I know how that sounds. You want to probably pitch this book across the room and say, "Madison, what the hell - why would you ever say something like that?" But that was my truth at the time. I share it because there might be someone reading this book who feels the same way.

Never validate yourself based on your bank account because that's got nothing to do with your value. Just because someone has a beautiful house and a swank car and diamonds on their hands doesn't mean they're rich - they might be in debt up to their eyeballs - their net worth might be lower than yours. Just because you see someone online posting pics of their vacations and private jets and parties they attend doesn't mean a thing—you know there are so many ways to fake a picture. Hell, there are businesses now that let you come in and take your picture in an airplane's first-class seating section, so your Facebook friends will think you're a hot hit. ("That'll show *you*, Carol Ann! And screw you for being a bitch in sixth grade.")

The fallout of this thinking is that it will affect who you associate with, and who you associate with is a prime factor in the opportunities that become available to you. If you won't approach a certain group of people because you're not "rich enough" to fit in, you're undermining your chances. You *must* associate with those very people, to get into those bigger opportunities, to step into the bigger life you are looking for. If you avoid the rich people until you become a rich person, then it probably will never happen for you. You don't get offered the chance to be part of million-dollar deals when you're hanging out at the QuikTrip drink station choosing between lime or lemon for your 32 ounces of iced tea.

Waiting for validation means just that: waiting. Go where you want to be, act like the person you want to be, show up in the places where things are happening, and walk in like you totally belong there.

### Wake Up Ready (a Diet and Exercise Philosophy)

Yeah, I know this chapter is about believing in yourself, and now I'm dropping this "fitness" section on you. You must admit though, that when you like how you look and feel, your confidence level goes up. But there's more to being "ready" for life than being able to fit into your high-school jeans or bench-press your own weight. I'm talking about being the person you want to be, starting right now. So, let's dish.

First, a disclaimer: This is not a book about how to diet or how to exercise. I'm not a fitness guru. I'm not a dietician. I wasn't even certain about including this because my whole perspective is about removing obstacles from your path – and sometimes obsessing over our bodies can be a huge obstacle.

What's kinda screwed up about this, is that it's obvious to me that fitness is so key, and I always felt great once I left the gym after a terrific workout. But it doesn't matter how much I love being in shape, I still find it difficult to drag my ass to the gym sometimes. My mom even bought one of those Peloton bikes which was a great idea, but then I just started making up excuses not to go to her living room.

Maybe I had the wrong motivations for going. *I look fat. I look bloated. I must fit into my clothes.* All this self-criticism, again - like going to the gym was some kind of punishment for my shortcomings.

What worked for me was changing my perception about workouts. I decided, "I'm going to look forward to exercise. I'm not making up for some deficiency. I'm doing this because it makes me feel great and strong and ready to take on any shit the world throws at me." I made myself remember gratitude for being physically able to work out and enjoy all the things my body could do. I made myself remember how lucky I am to live in a place where I have access to food that is good for me. I found the joy in readiness and good health. I discovered how much I needed to do to keep the level of health I want, and in doing so, became able to moderate myself, so that I'm not exhausting, starving, or tormenting myself.

Normalizing, appreciating, and living your diet and fitness regimen is so important because if you don't:

- you'll go overboard, putting in pointless time and effort, or
- you'll wait for some event to motivate you to get fit and healthy, or

- (the most likely option) you'll waffle back and forth between the two extremes.

## Going Overboard

If you don't find this balance, you'll get these obsessive weeks or months – these times when you put your life on hold to achieve an arbitrary goal. You can't let the size of your waist interfere with creating memories. I've done this - what I mean is, looking back, I think, "I wish I'd spent more Friday nights out before long weekends." But I was so obsessed with going to the gym. A long weekend meant going to the gym twice—on Friday and on Saturday morning, and it turns out that extra day didn't make any difference at all. I could have gone out and made some memories, but instead, I was in the gym stair-mastering to Bruno Mars.

## Waiting for Inspiration

Putting your life "on hold" for anything is a bad idea – because that "on hold" is in your imagination. Life keeps right on happening, whether you're tuned in for it or not. Pause buttons only work for your streaming service.

## Or Waffling...

Problem is, when you're not obsessively dieting or working out, you're tormenting yourself about how much you should be dieting or working out. Life is too short to waste it believing you should be doing something else.

## Understanding What is Right for YOU

Everyone is built differently. There's always this drive to conform to the current body fashion - let's all mimic Gwyneth or Kim or Scarlett. But really, I want you to be fit and healthy for your own benefit, not someone else's, and I want you to look like yourself, not someone else. We need to decide. What is "fit" for me? What is "healthy" for me? What makes *me* feel good?

Being thin or shredded or hot or cut is not going to solve your problems. It's kind of like having money, though. Having money is not the secret to happiness, but boy howdy, does it help clear those obstacles. It takes a load off your mind when you can make rent and keep the lights on and you aren't worried about getting your kneecaps busted by a collector named Ace— or worse, Citibank reps. In the same way, having good physical fitness is not the secret of a happy life, but it makes everything else that much easier. *It clears obstacles.* If you feel good, clear-headed, energetic, well-rested, and you like how you look, you just got bonus points toward making the rest of your goals come true.

Fitness must be a lifestyle, just like everything else in this book. It's about transforming your overall mindset and removing those obstacles that are holding you back from what you need to achieve. Fitness doesn't have to mean perfection by Instagram model standards. It does mean that physically, you can get up and get out and do the things you want to do, without exhausting yourself or popping six ibuprofen a day.

My first recommendation is taking yourself to the experts. Help is out there– take advantage of it. If your body cannot properly function, no self-help book is going to do you much good.

See a dietitian, an allergist, or a nutritionist– it's your call– but find out if there's anything in your diet that's going to cause you problems or be of great benefit to you. What's good for you, your blood type, your body shape?

Get your physical health and hormonal situation worked out. As you age, your body throws some curveballs at you. You can move through life for months or years feeling kinda terrible, believing it's all about your decisions and your emotions and your day-to-day when actually, it's about estrogen or testosterone or any one of the chemicals your body produces too much or too little of. Suffering from whacked-out hormones is just putting yourself at a disadvantage that makes everything else harder.

I highly recommend seeing private practice doctors, if at all possible, because they are more likely to fix you than medicate you. This is an investment in yourself, so you can live your best life, and it's cheaper than therapy!

When you feel well, you gain confidence. Gain confidence, and your mind opens. With an open mind, countless opportunities flow to you. Feeling good is the first step to attracting things in life.

I know, so many times I felt so insecure, so bogged down, just hiding behind this second wife, talking-trophy face, and I would just struggle, or I would feel nervous because I wasn't feeling good on the inside. When I *was* feeling good on the inside, it was just amazing how everything seemed to go so much easier.

### Diet and Fitness are Opportunities, Not Obstacles

What's worked for me, and I think might work for you, is remembering that *your life is happening right now.* Not in the future, after you've lost five pounds. It's happening today, whether you're thin or shredded or hot or cut. All the experts will tell you the present is peace, the past is depression, and the future is anxiety. So, your life is happening now. Why not look and feel your best *now*? Start thinking that way, and you'll discover that your exercise habits and diet fall right in line.

That means no more of this crap. "I must look great for this (wedding, event, party, high school reunion), so I need to go on this diet and eat this weird frickin' food and do all these weird rituals for the next two months, so I can show up, prove to Carol Ann that I'm doing better than her, and then I can go hork down a cheesecake to reward myself!"

Nope. Realize that the present, where you're standing right this moment, is about readiness. Adopt a lifestyle that knows, on any day, you can wake up ready for the biggest moment of your life. Because that's how life works. Life doesn't push the "hold" button to give you a month to lose ten pounds and then send that big opportunity around again. Besides, these "future" goals - I need to lose "x" amount of weight, I need to squeeze into this size 0 dress - that's just pushing opportunity out further into the future. I know this because I did it to myself over and over again.

When I was doing acting and comedy all the time, they always wanted to take headshots. I crash dieted, and did all these unhealthy things, like only eat grapes for two days and then work out like crazy and then drink a gallon of water. Then, after the headshots, I ate too much, felt guilty, and beat myself up. Just this constant vicious cycle. I even turned down an opportunity or two because I didn't like the way I looked, thinking things like "I can't do that until I lose five pounds." Was I using that five pounds as an excuse? Did I really think life would wait around for me to crash diet? The point is, I got in my own way, creating obstacles that stopped me from enjoying opportunities.

Fitness and diet are part of life, not something you do in an emergency. Live so that you never miss an opportunity because "I can't do that until I lose X pounds," or "I'm too tired to go out today," or "I'm too crazed on Twinkies to think straight." You should always be ready for what's coming at you. Wake up each morning like it's going to be the biggest day of your life: act like it and look like it in the way that works best for you.

## Ditching that Inner Critic

We're hard on ourselves because we don't want others to see us fail. This used to happen to me a lot in stand-up comedy. After a set, if I didn't feel it went well, even if people would say, "Nice set, Madison!" and they weren't talking about my ta-tas, I'd just shrug and say, "Eh, the audience hated me, I could have done a lot better, I wish I had done blah blah blah."

Finally, some friends pointed out what I was doing. "Why you gotta be so hard on yourself? It's the nature of comedy – you can do exactly the same thing every night, and shit will sometimes go great, or shit will sometimes go bad."

It didn't sink in though. I kept looking for that outside validation, for someone to say, "You are fantastic! Wow, I laughed so hard I peed everywhere, Madison, you're the funniest person ever."

Problem is, if someone had actually said that, the overly critical inner voice inside me would have doubted it, or told me it wasn't enough. "Well sure, that one doofus likes me, but everyone else thinks I suck." That inner critic loved to say, "I'm not good enough, or funny enough, and your family and friends know you're a failure. It's *really* obvious."

We just want to be "the best," but someone always seems to be better. Maybe we're not where we wanted to be by this time in our lives. That was always my deal. I thought I'd be rich and successful by age 26, but I wasn't. Then, I started creating all these obstacles in my own mind, getting in my own way. "I'm such a loser. Look at all my friends, they're all rich and living fantastic lives because they did shit the right way, but oh no, not me."

We fall into blame as a way of justifying the failures that we are sure will come soon. That negativity is contagious. It will have its way if we let it.

I'm telling you this now, so you don't have to wait until you're middle-aged to figure it out for yourself (and some people never figure it out anyway). You cannot be loved by everyone. The things you do will never please everyone. Even those closest to you – your Mom, your bestie, the love of your life – may not love what you're doing. That doesn't mean what you're doing is wrong, or that they will stop loving *you*. It means you're following your own path. Now, that's a liberating thought! All you must do is remind that nasty little jackass in your head, the one who criticizes you all the time, that you don't need his/her help any longer.

It's important that you validate yourself because you cannot wait around for the world to validate you - to hand you that job, tell you you're smart enough, pump that number into your bank account, get you into the "right" crowd.

Love what you do, including the mistakes you make, because it is all serving your path and your purpose. Don't forever be chasing compliments and reassurances. Validate yourself. Be honest and grateful for your efforts and opportunities. "I worked my ass off on that. I did the best job I could do. I rocked that – I did better this time than last time, and next time, I'll do even better. Hell yeah." Here's what inner validation is going to do for you:

- It's the only validation you *need*. It's okay to want outside validation to a reasonable extent – that's how we get jobs and raises and circles of friends…but inner validation is what will keep you going forward when outside validation is nowhere to be found.

- Inner validation will shut up that inner critic. "You're not good enough," the little whisper will say, and you'll shout back, *"I'm sorry, I can't hear you while I'm kicking ass and taking names!"*

- Inner validation lets you know your own worth – and that means you will never "chase" again. You will come at opportunities with the ability to walk away the moment it seems like anyone in that room doesn't see your value. The power to walk away from anything – a relationship, a business deal, a job, a conflict – is the power to dictate your terms. You don't have to put up with bullshit, prove yourself time and again, or clean up after people like you're pledging some bitchy sorority. If there is an opportunity you want, express your abilities, express your interest, express your strategy. But be willing to shrug and say, "That's okay, never mind – life has something else in mind for me." P.S. – often, when you stop chasing, you will find yourself being chased.

### Summary

Believing in yourself, living your health and fitness goals, and telling your inner critic to get lost all takes active effort on your part. It starts with recognizing where your fears and problems manifest.

So, let's say that job interview didn't go well. You were nervous, you laughed at all the wrong times, and you mistook the boss's boyfriend for her son. Great. Now, instead of beating yourself up on the train home about what a stupid loser you are (which gets you nowhere), try instead to think of what you learned from this experience and what you might be able to do in the future to curb your anxieties.

Look at your position from the outside – think how many people would admire or even envy you for trying the things you're trying, for being brave enough to put yourself on the line. And finally, try as hard as you can to find the humor in the situation because let's be honest – some of these situations make great stories later on. Life is funny. Time to lighten the fuck up.

# CHAPTER SEVEN

## TIME TO ESCAPE THE TUNNEL

### *The Perils of Tunnel Vision*

After Wall Street and the ecommerce business, when I decided to really follow my dream of being a comic, I did acting as well, because those things go together.

I fought so hard, telling myself, "I'm going to be a comedian. I'm going to be an actress." I wouldn't even consider options beyond those specific things. I don't even remember the idea of being a comic or an actress making me all that happy. I just thought it was something I needed to do because I couldn't have *three* failed careers.

But obviously, I had to make money somehow, especially when comedy wasn't paying. I worked temp job after temp job. Temping is like appearing on a daily reality show where you never know what's waiting for you. It means working for nice people, mean people, crazy people, so many different personalities. It means doing jobs that you never wanted to do, never imagined doing, maybe that you never even knew were actually "jobs." It means, sometimes, sucking it up because you're treated badly by people who know nothing about you. Some of these people would treat me like furniture, not even giving me the basic courtesy you'd extend to a human being. Hey, that was *their* problem, but it felt bad anyway.

This was the time when tunnel vision became a real problem for me. It compounded my scarcity mindset and made my problems harder to escape. I saw myself as having "failed" before and refused to "fail" again. Remember, that often what we call failure is not failure at all. It's a pivot, a redirection, a course correction, but not failure.

I was so obsessed that I never imagined that my actual success and happiness would come from a different angle.

As a comic and an actress, of course I had a manager who tried really hard to promote my career for me. After we'd worked together for some time, my manager told me, "You're a really good creator. You should look at creating and producing."

My first response was to take it as a personal insult, thinking that he meant: *You're not pretty enough or special enough to be on TV.*

But once I was finally able to listen to him, removing that tunnel vision of "I have to be an actress/comedian," it opened my mind to other options of how to make money, and I suddenly realized that so many opportunities surrounded me.

In fact, opportunities started piling up everywhere in multiple ways. I realized I could make money in dozens of ways that bring me happiness. I could have a career in entertainment, yes, but on the other side of the camera: development, writing, producing, and creating.

Now, I am open to everything. I create reality television shows. I'm working on a movie, and on this book series. I am a public speaker, I work with cryptocurrency, and I have a self-help/business podcast where I get to speak with fascinating, brilliant guests. Would I have ever been able to open myself up to these experiences if I were still obsessed with thinking that I couldn't be anything but a "famous stand-up comic?" Probably not.

So, let's imagine you went to college for fashion design. You got out, you started working in fashion, making your way rung by rung up the "fashion ladder." Five or ten or twenty years later, it occurs to you that you're stalled out somewhere in the fashion industry, and it feels like you're going nowhere, or maybe you don't even like it, and you think, "Fantastic. I should have made a completely different decision back in college."

But now you're stuck. This is all you can do for the rest of your life, might as well just deal with it because now you have a 401(k), and a dog with Lyme disease who needs dog meds, and you're sure nobody else will pay you this much money to do anything else because you don't know how to do anything else. You feel like you must be the best at "this" or nothing else matters. You've got to have a Jaguar, a Roomba, and perfect teeth, or you're sucking at life, and by God, this is how you're gonna get it.

That tunnel toward freedom or reward looks long and dark, doesn't it? The thing is, nobody's keeping you in there but yourself. There you sit, with a world of potential and talent inside you. You've spent so much time resenting this job and regretting your decisions that you've failed to notice what you're gaining: experience, expertise, connections, maturity - and that's just for starters. Unbeknownst to you, you're becoming an expert, but you wouldn't notice an opportunity if it bit you on the ass. Imagine yourself for a moment doing something new - taking all that fabulous know-how and offering it up to the Universe to see what comes rolling happily back to you.

In the back of your mind, you want more: another job, another project, another place to live. But you're attached to the outcome of staying at this job. *Ugh. Well, I've already adapted to this lifestyle. I can't do anything else. What if it doesn't work out? What if I lose all this safety? What if blah-dee-blah-dee-blah?* Yep, and then anything else that you could be doing drifts right by you. Nobody offers you chances or jobs or anything else because they see you, closed off, unwilling to try. And that safety you feel is an illusion, I'm sorry to say. Nothing in life is guaranteed. That sucky job can disappear in a heartbeat.

All that may sound kind of obvious, but you wouldn't believe how many tunnel-dwellers I speak to who respond with, "I can't do that, I can't make a change, I can't just…switch shit up like that!"

Not with that attitude, you can't!

Feeling trapped or stuck like this, is all about suffering a case of tunnel vision. You've done the same thing for so long that you can't really imagine doing anything else. You're afraid of losing the steady money, and I get that, but there are so many other ways to make money, both actively and passively.

And maybe you'll find a better career, in something else, something you hadn't thought of before. Maybe you're in a network with someone who wants to start a sunscreen company and they see a set of skills in you that would fit brilliantly with their plans. Tunnel vision will make you say, "No, I work in fashion, I have a fashion degree, I'm on the fashion ladder."

There's a phenomenon out there called the "midlife career change." People hit an age somewhere between 40 and 60 and realize they're fed up with the jobs they've been doing since college. Hate is a strong word - they don't all hate their jobs, but they may be bored, burned out, or feeling unfulfilled somehow.

Well, chances are pretty good that those feelings started way back, years before, but when people hit middle age, they get braver because they realize, "Oh shit, I'm gonna die someday. If I want to do something amazing, I've got to go do it now."

They realize that it's time to crawl out of the tunnel and take in the 360-degree viewpoint. Suddenly, these people get super-cool, start traveling the world, saving lives, and solving mysteries. Like, you see your Aunt Judy at a family reunion and realize that she's turned into an amazing hybrid of Jane Goodall and Rick Steves and Janis Joplin, and now she's taking calls from billionaires and dating someone from the Eagles. "Didn't she used to be an insurance agent?" you ask Mom or Dad. "Yes, but then she made a career change," they respond. *Career change* seems like a pretty mild term for it— Aunt Judy left the tunnel behind, opened her horizons to what the Universe had to offer her, and is living her dream.

I'm suggesting you allow yourself to have this epiphany long before you hit middle age. Especially with the Internet linking us fast and free to, like, *everybody else*, you can look outside your tunnel for as many opportunities as you have the time and the desire for. You can explore to your heart's content and network with people around the globe.

But be smart and safe in your explorations - online or in person, beware of scammers, but don't let the idea of scammers stop you. Just remember to protect yourself, check sources, don't give out personal financial information and never offer or agree to send anyone money. If you want to learn how to avoid scammers, turn on Netflix and watch anything they've produced in the last eighteen months in what is apparently their "People Suck" series of programming materials. Then, you'll know to refuse, if someone tells you they are a spy, an heiress, or just offers you participation tickets to Squid Game.

## Practicing Non-Attachment

Something that keeps us stuck in tunnel vision is that deceptive "light at the end" of a project or goal that we are singularly devoted to, so much that we neglect our other options.

By all means, you gotta have goals, you gotta want things. That's key. But I'm saying it cannot be the *only* thing you are working toward. It will blind you to opportunity. If you believe that success means "this thing and this thing only," then you are suffering from attachment.

For a while, I believed I had to be a comic/actress and refused to consider other options. Then, I developed this obsession with making a movie. I wrote a film, and I kept trying to get it made, and get it made, and nothing ever happened. I let this hurt me for too long. I had to get out of the mindset that it was "this movie or nothing." I had to say, "If the movie gets made, fantastic. And if it doesn't, that's okay because so many other things are happening for me now."

When you have a success, they're going to be asking. "What else is ready to go?" Wouldn't it be better to actually have something ready? Once I escaped the tunnel vision, removed my attachment to that project alone, I felt this huge sense of relief and the joy of success. Now, I have so many projects in the works, so many things progressing and paying off, that something is always happening. I'm not forced to pin all my hopes (and energy) on one thing.

So, here we go again, with the "too much of a good thing" problem. Am I suggesting you have so many irons in the fire, so many projects, that you never get anything completed? That you live in a constant state of stress and tension because you can't get a damn thing done and you've got more work than you can handle? Of course not.

If anything, opening your horizons should give you the chance to work on exactly what you want and drop the projects that don't mean anything to you or that aren't going anywhere. You can finish one project, or get it to the point where the ball is in someone else's court, and instead of biting your nails and pacing the floor waiting to see what happens, you've got something else to occupy your thoughts, something else to look forward to.

Excessive attachment gives off a stench. When you want something desperately, other people know it. You walk into the pitch, interview, meeting, phone call, first date—whatever—reeking of neediness, and this is problematic for so many reasons. You're anxious and jittery, you're second-guessing everything, saying all the wrong stuff. You'll do whatever they ask you to do to make shit happen, and you usually end up with the short end of the stick or, worse, you scare people off completely.

Look, have you ever gone into a situation where you just didn't really care that much, one way or the other? Maybe you got a job interview someplace you'd never seriously considered working. That interview was probably one of the best you ever did, because you were sooo chill. Nobody intimidated you. You didn't really think twice about what anyone thought. Suddenly, they're falling all over themselves to try to get you interested in the job. Or maybe not—maybe everybody realized this wasn't meant to be, and you all happily went your separate ways. But you weren't attached to the idea of this job, and it just took the whole situation down a thousand decibels.

Some of my best nights have been the nights where somebody just said, "Let's go grab a drink." Maybe I was like, "Okay, whatever, like I washed my hair two days ago and I don't have any makeup on, and I just got back from the gym and haven't washed my hoo-ha, but who cares. We're just going to grab a drink."

And it ends up being one of the best nights ever. I even find I get hit on more when I look like shit. Why? Because I take that wall down. I don't think anybody is going to hit on me, and I have no expectations. Suddenly, I'm the coolest bitch in the room.

*But Madison, does this mean I should act like I don't care about anything?* No, and by now, you should know better than to ask! Kidding. It's just that "caring" and "desperation" are not the same. It is possible to care, express interest, and invest yourself in situations without coming at them like the guys at Comic-Con latched onto the model in Princess Leia's gold bikini.

Of course, you don't want to be a walking disaster, never showering or checking a mirror or bothering to be polite. But people can be great at what they do without it meaning *everything* to them. Love what you do, but keep your attachment at a level that you know you will be okay even if things don't work out. Your plans and goals are flexible, interrelated, they feed each other and help each other, and you. Remember when we talked about the ability to "walk away" when things weren't ideal for your path? That's exactly what this is about.

## Summary

Tunnel vision is only good for bats and train conductors. For you, it just means missed experiences and opportunities. Don't focus so hard on any single thing, person, job, way of life, accomplishment, goal, or image of yourself that you can't see an incredible doorway when it opens.

From the time we are corralled into school, we're taught about hard work and perseverance and "stick-to-it-iveness." We hear stories about people who focused intensely on success in some area and sacrificed everything for their goals. We admire these people. We're told that nothing is out of reach if we work hard enough, and then we're told to get back to work.

What we aren't taught is that it's fine – in fact, it's mentally healthy – to avoid attaching yourself too much to a be-all-end-all importance to one very specific thing. That's called obsession. It's not just a perfume. Remember that you are more than a single goal or title. As you work toward making your dreams come true, open your eyes to *all* the things you can have and be.

# CHAPTER EIGHT

## TIME TO STOP BEING OFFENDED

### *I've Seen a Lot of Dicks*

One sunny day in February in 2003, I was 20 years old, still in college, slouching around campus like everyone else and trying to find my way into the ultimate spring break.

I came across this wonderful travel agency called BJ's Travel, and they said they could give me a discount, where for only $1,500, my friend Ashley and I could go and stay for a week at an all-inclusive, five star-resort in Jamaica. Even the flight was included! There was this awesome sense of mystery too, because we wouldn't know exactly where we were staying until we got there. That must be how they managed to keep the prices so low.

I said, "Perfect! Sign me up!"

My dad, the accountant, probably impressed that I'd done my research and was being so economical, paid for the trip.

Once they had my information, BJ's contacted me to ask a simple question. "Are you okay with a topless beach?"

Ta-tas didn't scare me. I said, "Sure, no problem!"

Ashley and I flew down on a plane loaded with partygoing spring-breakers. We landed in Montego Bay, and all of us kids piled out with our duffle bags and beach towels and flipflops a'floppin. Outside the terminal, all the college kids seemed to be jumping on these colorful fun buses with bass riffs pounding out the windows.

Ashley and I looked around, and looked at each other, until someone instructed us, "You're on *that* bus." And holy crap! Everyone on board was so much older than us. It looked like we were vacationing with our *parents*! But this was our ride, so we jumped on the bus.

We got to the hotel, and we checked in. They said, "Just wait in the lobby. Feel free to order drinks from the bar, and when your room is ready, we'll escort you up."

As we wandered away towards the bar, we began noticing some décor that was just rather fleshy, bulbous, erm, objects d'art, you might say, that were out of the ordinary. I remember tile mosaics that looked like pictures out of the *Kama Sutra*...but we didn't really think anything of it yet. We saw there was no one at the pool. That seemed pretty strange. This was supposed to be an exciting place. Were we the first ones to arrive?

We ordered Bahama Mamas, one of those spring break drinks with tons of calories because we still had a metabolism back then.

Drink in hand, I looked over to my right, and saw a long, very limp cock just waving in the wind, and it happened to be attached to stark naked, 40-something man who was strolling by like this was just ordinary life for him. As he was well-endowed, his dick swung back and forth like a pendulum as he passed us. I don't think I'd ever seen a limp dick at that point in my life.

Astonished, Ashley and I fell out laughing.

The bartender noticed our surprise and asked, "Do you all know where you're at?" Because apparently, we did not. He said, "You're at Hedonism II. *The Land Where Anything Goes.*"

"What does that mean?" I asked.

He said, "It's wet and wild - basically you're at a nudist swingers' colony."

But I said, "What does *that* mean?" I had been raised by a good Christian family; the topic of swinging had never come up outside a playground. A *kids'* playground.

The naked man said, "Well, you're in luck. This is the Prude Side. Over *there* is the Nude Side. That's where you'll find more of the fun. But don't worry. Nobody's going to harass you or force you to do anything."

And he was right. People couldn't have been nicer or more respectful, though our presence didn't stop them from doing what they'd come there to do. Word got around that we had wound up at Hedonism II by accident, and as soon as they saw that Ashley and I were going to live and let live, everyone just found it funny.

We spent seven days at the wildest party in Jamaica. The participants were all happy to answer our questions and let us take it all in...er, I mean...watch as much as we wanted. Or as little as we wanted. I was a young woman in college, so I had seen porn before, but in porn, the participants can't make eye contact with you. Believe me, that makes it a whole new thing.

So, we had the Prude Side, where we could relax and be ourselves, but we'd go over to the Nude Side for some good stories. Besides, the Nude Side had all the best drinks and food. I was just careful to never sit *anywhere* without putting a towel down first.

Thus, I have seen every size orifice that you could imagine. I saw things I can never unsee. Twenty years old and I'd seen a thousand dicks in one week.

I even watched an interactive game of dice – oh, face it, *all* the games were interactive. One die named body parts on each side, and the other die had action verbs, and pairs of people would roll to see who was doing what to whom. Everyone just went for it. These people were fearless and absolutely accepting of each other. *Really* accepting.

And I even took part – well, just in the wet t-shirt contest – but still, I got on board for the fun. Weird having a wet t-shirt contest at a nudist swinger's party. All these great tits bouncing around and now they want to put shirts on? Maybe after you get used to bare flesh, clothes start feeling pretty kinky.

But the greatest part of this resort is that you could go down the waterslide buck-naked. If you've never done that, I'm telling you, put it on your bucket list. There is no drag. For ladies, it is the best public douche you will ever have. You may never need another for the rest of your life.

The funniest thing was coming home to tell Mom and Dad about it. "How was spring break?" they naturally asked me. And I said, "Unbelievable! I was at Hedonism II."

*Whoosh*, it went right over Dad's head. He didn't understand the implications until he mentioned it to a client at his accounting office. "Oh yes, you know, my daughter just came back from Jamaica. She went to Hedonism II."

Apparently, the look on the client's face was alarming. "Excuse me…you sent your daughter to Hedonism II?"

Dad's smile faltered. "Um – why? What is it?"

So yeah, I had to answer a few more questions that evening. But Dad and Mom were cool about the whole thing. Though my family was Christian, we were never shy about dirty jokes. You should have heard some of the things said over Christmas dinner. Next year, my dad was saying, "Madison, tell them all about your spring break!" So now, I just had another outrageous experience that made us all laugh. It really was the gift that kept on giving.

Now there are plenty of self-help books that will tell you to step outside your comfort zone to broaden your horizons. I think Hedonism II was about as far outside my comfort zone as I had ever been. Maybe it didn't broaden my personal horizons, but it taught me something really valuable about people and perceptions.

What I learned from that experience – that I can mention in mixed company - is that just because it's not your lifestyle, and just because people are very different from you, doesn't mean you should judge. We met a lot of wonderful people who respected our boundaries and welcomed our curiosity. I guess that shouldn't be surprising. If ever a bunch of people needed to be open-minded, it was the participants of Hedonism II. I've carried the lesson with me ever since that Spring Break: open your mind, open your heart. Remember that every crazy thing that happens, will be a great story you can use to make people laugh for the rest of your life.

## Everybody's Offended

There are at least three different ways that offense can come at you, and I want to talk about all of them, and tell you why it's time to lighten the fuck up on how offended we are. Let's break it down.

## When We Disagree

### Case One: Someone said something that upset me because I don't agree with it.

The media is creating and causing problems that make us more sensitive to certain things that maybe we shouldn't really be sensitive to. They are driving a fear narrative and brainwashing us at the same time. We get so consumed by this, that we start to lose sense of who we are.

I hope that in the future, this is no longer true. But political affiliation is a huge problem right now (2022), polarizing us, confusing us – and the thing is, everyone is raised with different values, experiences, and education. Political alignment is incredibly controversial, and the media is driving us to "hate" people who disagree with us. Hate destroys you. The next time you find yourself becoming enraged about some else's opinion, remember that love gets more done. The media has convinced you that what others believe is so much more extreme and dangerous than it is. Diversity of thought is an incredible resource in our world. We need to encourage it.

Remember, the media's job is to promote fear. It's probably not in their mission statement (or heck, I don't know, maybe it is) but promoting fear is what gets you to keep tuning in, listening to what they say, buying their products, following their advice. Fear gets people moving and reacting; being offended is very much like being afraid, only it feels better because you can claim to be angry and strong, instead of pissing-your-britches scared and helpless. The minute you can disconnect from the media—mentally or otherwise, you regain your control. Either "turn it off" or "tune it out." Disengage. You don't have to believe everything you hear, and you don't have to take everything you hear so dead seriously.

Let yourself laugh at some things. Comedy is in danger of being cancelled out of existence, and we need it to live. If we can't laugh at ourselves, if we can't develop the mental resilience to laugh at the bizarre, stupid things than happen on Planet Earth, we're in a lot of trouble. When you are offended, it does terrible things to your body. Your heart races, your brain races—you can't make good decisions. We need that offensive funny humor where we can actually sit back and go, "Hey, that wasn't so bad. What was I so offended by? What was I so sensitive about? Those were just words. By hearing them, I didn't have to agree with them, nor believe them."

Here's a harsh truth: if you can't stand to hear someone disagreeing with you, it's because you don't have faith in your own beliefs. People get the most offended by things that make them doubt their beliefs and their faith. They are offended by ideas that confront their own personal issues, and fears they haven't worked out yet. If you are secure in your beliefs and faith, things have far less power to disturb or offend you.

## When Things Go Wrong for Us

### Case Two: Someone did something that inconvenienced or perturbed me.

It's because we take things personally—like really, seriously, drama-queen personally. We think that everything is about us, when in reality, it's not. Very little is about you. Everyone in the world thinks that they are just as important as you think you are. To be fair, we can't help it—we only live inside our own heads, we only know what happens to us. But to be even more fair, once you realize that 99.9999 percent of the world is happening around you and not *to* you, your life will get a lot more chill.

Not everyone thinks the way you do. We were all raised differently; our minds work differently. We all aspire to different things. Try to remember this when someone misunderstands you, does not comprehend your big picture, fails to pay what you think are the proper respects. Think of it from your own perspective. How many times have you *purposely* set out to offend someone during your everyday life?

Probably not many. Most of the time when we cut someone off in traffic, make too much noise, say the wrong thing, serve the wrong drinks, forget to return the thing we borrowed, tag someone as older or younger or more pregnant than they actually are, it's just a thoughtless mistake. We're distracted and forgetful. We screw up sometimes. So, the next time you decide to get personally pissed because someone "did something to you," try and consider. Did they "do something to you," or did something just happen, and you were in the way? Did it *really* have anything to do with you?

### When Something Really is Offensive

*Case Three: Yeah, but sometimes PEOPLE ARE JERKS. There is still that 0.0001 percent of the time when it truly feels like it's ALL ABOUT YOU.*

Well, it's still not all about you. It takes two to be offended - yourself and the person who offended you, and yeah, they may be a real piece of work. That's not your problem. You don't have to fix them or accommodate them. Laugh it off.

I remember the first time I was told I had a "rich face." Was this a compliment? Being rich is fun - I wanted to be rich. So, I felt flattered. But wait: I *wasn't* rich at the time, so I felt a little offended. What did that even mean? It meant somebody said something kind of dumb, and now I was worried. If I have a rich face, does that mean I look like I already have all my shit together? Now how is anyone ever going to know that I'm struggling and need this gig, this job, this opportunity? So, I imagined a hundred ways that having a "rich face" was going to ruin my life, and I got mad and worried.

What I needed to do is just laugh it off. Luckily, as a comedian, I worked it out. I put it into a joke. I said, "Instead of resting bitch face, I have resting rich face, which ain't so bad. I just need my bank account to catch up."

Next time you get offended, I encourage you just to step back, take a deep breath, have a laugh, and think, "Well, I gotta admit it's kind of funny." I've been called a lot of names, suffered a lot of judgments. People assume a lot of things about me - but that's true for everyone. You don't know what another person has been through, you don't know their thoughts or intentions, whether they are seething with envy, seriously confused, or honestly out of their skulls.

I remember one day in New York City, I was bringing my lunch back to one of my temp jobs. I was just standing on the corner waiting for the light so I could cross, and I was totally minding my own business. An older gentleman stood nearby, in a suit and trench coat. He could have been friends with my dad. The light changed, and this man passed me then stopped and turned. Looking me dead in the face, he said, "Bitch."

*What?* Please, that's so stupid it's crazy – he didn't know a thing about me. Something about me triggered some nasty old shit in his head. Not my problem. So, I said, "Oh, I'm sorry, I must look like your ex-wife," and I just kept on walking. It was just a word. I didn't let him have the power to hurt me with it. In fact, I was able to come back with a joke that made me laugh.

Just understand that you are on your own journey. What you choose to be offended by is up to you. And the more offended you let yourself become, the more anxious and unhappy you will feel. The ones you're harming are yourself and the people who care about you.

### Taking the High Road

Let's talk a moment about diffusing difficult situations. This is a key element of lightening the fuck up, because not everybody has lightened the fuck up. There are people out there who are so angry, pissy, envious, constipated – hell if I know what's wrong with them – that they will say and do all kinds of offensive shit. Maybe they'll do it outright, maybe they'll be passive aggressive about it, but their goal is the same. They want to hurt you. Maybe they want to start a fight. They would love for you to get defensive and angry in return. Some of these trolls aren't content until they believe everyone is as unhappy as they are.

Sometimes, that's not the case. You will, in fact, bump into people on the wrong day, after they've been in the wrong meeting, or been dumped, or gotten a lousy review, or they've mistaken you for the bully who used to throw food at them in the lunchroom.

And let me tell you, I have a face that people like to judge. I've gone through this my whole life. Females weren't very nice to me at first, so I learned to diffuse situations by putting it out there as fast as I can. "I may look like I'm about to trash you on Instagram, but I'm a cool chick who likes beer and dick jokes." I even had a friend who once told me, "I hated you at first, because you reminded me of every Upper East Side, stuck-up rich bitch I've had a bad experience with." Um, *thanks?* I remember saying, "What the heck is the Upper East Side? I'm from Colorado."

But this is the way of it: we make first-impression judgments; we can't always help the first thing that pops into our heads. So, if you run into someone who is problematic, my advice would be to give them the benefit of the doubt, and the way you do this is by *diffusing the situation*. Be the bigger person – but don't be cocky about it. Here are some ways to diffuse:

1) Apologize. Yeah, even if it wasn't your fault. If it's something trivial, just say, "Whoops, my bad, oh well." It's not unusual for someone to hear you apologize and wake up to reality. "Oh shit, no, that was my fault." And suddenly, you're having a conversation with a human.

2) Own up to mistakes at once and honestly. Don't make excuses. Don't try covering shit up. "Yes, I messed up. What can I do to fix it?" Some of the craziest arguments I've ever heard involved people trying to wiggle their way out of blame. "How was I supposed to know that the front door opened *and* closed? It's not labeled. I wasn't trained for doors. I have a condition that makes me door-blind."

3) Be nice. This is pretty simple. I think it's probably the first thing anyone ever told you about relationships.

4) Have a sense of humor. Nothing diffuses anger and frustration faster than laughter.

Here's an example of a situation I was involved in that I had to quickly diffuse. I went to the Hamptons with a group of friends. We arrived in a room, and I flicked on the lights, only to discover I woke up a woman who was sleeping on a bed. She was angry, tired, and looking for a fight.

Now, what I could have said was, "What's your problem, chica?" I'm tired too, you know. What I did instead was...

1) Apologize. "Oops, I'm so sorry!"

2) Own up to mistakes. "My bad. I had no idea you were in here, or I wouldn't have done that."

3) Be nice. "I'll even unpack in the other room."

4) Have a sense of humor. "You can wake me up anytime you want; I won't be mad."

Did I *want* to say all that? Not really. But I did it anyway. It worked out really well in my favor. We were able to get past a bad first impression into a pretty sweet acquaintanceship—turned out she ran the door of one of the hottest clubs in the Hamptons. Guess who was getting to the front of the line and getting free drinks? *Me!*

We all want to stick up for ourselves. We all want to be right. But sometimes it's better to stop and think, "What am I really getting out of this? What am I really going to accomplish by being mad? Is this a 'win' that's going to matter in the long run?"

If you're trying to diffuse a situation while dealing with a real asshole, most of these suggestions won't work. That's how you know the difference between the assholes and someone who's just having a bad day. I'm not sure it matters though, because nothing makes an asshole angrier than someone who refuses to stoop to their level. So, by taking the high road, you've got the win/win situation of looking like the hero and also getting a little revenge, too. Hey, I never said I was an angel.

### Summary

All right, students of 'Time To Lighten The Fuck Up.' Let us review what we have learned in this chapter.

- Sometimes, we get offended when people don't agree with us. That is a preposterous waste of time and energy. Every human being on this planet has infinite ways to be different from you – and somewhere in all that infinity, you can usually find some common ground. Life's too short to argue and be angry about stupid things, especially when it's just talk. Be the champ who saves Thanksgiving for your poor family. If you're around people who aren't mature enough to handle disagreement, to have a sincere conversation about differing opinions, then switch the topic to ice cream, which is something most people can agree on, unless, of course, they're lactose intolerant.

- Sometimes, we get offended because we are inconvenienced or we feel that we've been treated unfairly. Well, first, put on your thinking cap and figure out if there is really a problem or if you're just getting bent out of shape over nothing. If there really is a problem, don't sit around being angry. Be the agent for change. You'll get a whole lot more done.

- Sometimes, things really are offensive. Okay, yes – but save yourself some grief by figuring out whether it's worth getting upset about. It takes two, you know – if you refuse to let yourself be affected by someone's stupid remarks or actions, it's a victory for your side of the argument.

- Sometimes, we need to take the high road, and be the bigger person, even when technically, we're not at fault, or we kinda have a good reason to be pissed. Pick your battles. Save your energy for the shit that really matters. Let some things slide, and you might find your actions have a really positive influence on the people around you.

And I'd like to remind you that words can't hurt unless you let them. For example, the language in this book is kinda rough. Let's just say, I've got a certain number of "fucks" to give – precisely 24, in fact. Sorry! But sometimes certain language is needed to drive a point home. If you're letting my 24 f-bombs offend you, then I'd like to say, "Thanks for reading my fucking book!"

# CHAPTER NINE

## TIME TO IMPROVE YOUR RELATIONSHIPS

### *Romantic Relationships*

I saw a marquis today for some entitled woman's prenuptial event. It said, "Welcome to Rachel's Bridal Brunch! 62 days until she says, 'I do!'"

I thought, *holy crap! She's having events two whole months before her wedding? Does she have some shit going on every weekend until she and her poor future husband tie the knot?* This kind of stuff amazes me. We celebrate weddings like these people are really carrying out something. It's not a skill to get married. I wish we'd celebrate other achievements with the same vigor. Rachel got her dream job? Rachel wrote a government-toppling manifesto? Rachel cured anal warts? Sure, I'll go to a brunch for those things.

It's not that I'm against marriage as an institution. I'm just baffled by how much our society overvalues and overplays the milestones of couple-relationships.

That being said, I'm not a relationship expert, nor do I want to be. I'm not qualified to tell you how to fall in love or have the perfect marriage. What I'm suggesting instead, is that, like everything else this book talks about, we could all lighten the fuck up when it comes to relationships.

We have made relationships stupidly, overly complicated when they're actually very simple. If you're questioning whether a person likes you, if you're not sure how they feel, if you're looking at your phone hoping they're going to text back, but you're just not sure...they're not right for you.

It isn't that "you're not good enough." It isn't that you've done something wrong (unless you, you know, stole their identify or something – don't do that shit!). Remember when we talked about rejection? There are infinite reasons why you don't click for someone else – and if you think about it, do you really want to be with someone who isn't crazy about you? Do you want to be "tolerated" or "settled for?" No way, and you deserve better than that. So, when you get the "stop" signal from someone – even if they seem like they would just be *perfect*, respect that, and quickly move on.

Society has put so much pressure on us individuals to find the right partner, get married, have kids, and play these expected roles. There is this weird stigma about spending "time alone." What kind of social leper is out there eating by herself or going to a party alone or spending Valentine's Day solo-drooling over *Avengers* movies? (Little secret for you – plenty of "coupled" people envy that freedom.)

Anyhow, you don't have to do any of it – what you need to do is what makes your heart happy. If your heart seeks a marriage, then do that – awesome. But if your heart isn't in that, you don't have to. It's a heartwarming thought, this idea that there is a person we can spend our lives with, but we place far more emphasis on the idea than it calls for. We overthink it and push ourselves to conform to this idea, so we make mistakes and jump into relationships we're not ready for – and in doing so, we're involving not just our own lives, but the lives of others.

No, I get it – we want to pair up. We want the dream, and it feels urgent. Hey, my biological clock is ticking. I used to think that was some made up thing, but it's real. I'm at the point now, where I'm like *yeah, I'd settle.* I used to have a "Dealbreaker List." Now I have a "I-Can-Deal-With-It List." When I was in my 20s, I didn't want to meet your single friend unless he was a sexy, strong, impeccably groomed billionaire astronaut." Now, I'm like, "Does he have a face?"

Seriously though, people put so much pressure on themselves to find a relationship. And what really is a relationship? I guess it's being around someone who you feel comfortable sharing intimate conversation with and getting naked in front of occasionally. But if that's the case, I'm having a relationship with my gynecologist. And my dentist, but that's a whole other story.

But let's look at this from another angle. We see someone and what we see says "YES" a thousand times over, but we hesitate. "I can't talk to that person – what if they reject me? I won't be able to stand it." Well – yeah, you can. You can stand it.

The quickest way to get over the fear of rejection is to let it happen a few times and don't take it to heart. I'm able to get onstage with no makeup on, and talk about shaving my asshole in front of 300 people – no big deal – not even worried about it. You'd think that would pretty much sew up all my self-confidence issues.

But twenty minutes later, there's a cute guy in a bar who I'd like to talk to…oh my god, I shrivel up like an unshaven asshole. *Oh my god he'll hate me, he'll laugh at me, it's going to be terrible, I'll never get over the rejection…*God knows I was more terrified by what I imagined than anything that might actually happen.

When I finally forced myself to simply approach men to speak to them, here's what happened. Some guys said "No, thanks." Some guys said, "Sorry, already in a relationship…" Some said, "Yes," but I kinda wished I hadn't asked after all. So, what's the moral of the story? Rejection isn't lethal, and maybe also we make way too big a deal out of the prospect of just speaking to someone new.

Why? Because in a certain mindset, the "Omigod I gotta get into a relationship!" mindset, makes every new encounter come with this metric shit ton of stress. *Is this THE ONE? Could this be TRUE LOVE? Should we order the Bloomin' Onion, or is that too much like commitment? Maybe just the cheese sticks for now.*

That's not a euphemism for sex. And speaking of sex…

I'm going to offer a bit of sage advice. I can't tell you what to do with your body, but I think we jump too quickly into sex. If you want to have sex with a lot of people, that's your prerogative, but chasing sex is kinda like chasing money – be sure you're going after it for the right reasons. If you just love sex, and it makes you feel fantastic, that's terrific. Have as much consenting-adult sex as your crazy bod can handle; your body and mind are the ultimate playground.

BUT if you're chasing sex to fill a void, to cure loneliness, to make people like you, to "keep" someone from leaving you, to get even, to get presents, or if you're coming away from sex feeling bad about yourself, feeling used or empty, rethink what you're doing to yourself.

I have a therapist who once told me, "Women have a harder time randomly sleeping with men because something is being put into us, we're taking on a little bit of their DNA. Which means they could be injecting us with 300 years of family history and trauma."

I couldn't believe it. "Are you telling me that every time I have unprotected sex, I've potentially got the Industrial Revolution in my vagina? Because it doesn't feel like any of them are working that hard."

But I also see what she meant – women are more vulnerable when it comes to sex. We take a lot of risk into ourselves, in more ways than one, when we engage in sex. So, I just want to make sure that you – woman, man or other – are engaging in sex that makes you happy. It doesn't all have to be "the best sex you ever had," but it should at least be "better than just watching the Weather Channel," and it should *never* make you feel bad about yourself.

### *The Law of Attraction and Attraction*

Timing is a big issue when it comes to love. Are you ready to receive? With everything you do – a relationship is the same as that big job, that big break, that big business deal. Are you ready, are you in a position, and taking the actions you need, to make that happen? Look at your life. If you are doing everything you can for your business, fitness, and finances, but you are missing in the relationships area, if you're lacking (and this is still somewhat of a struggle for me) – then you can ask, "What am I doing that is leading me away from relationships?"

- *Do you have a negativity loop in your head? This is when you are so certain that you'll never meet the right person, so you stop trying.*

- *Do you find yourself easily annoyed by the people you meet? Are you being overly particular and demanding?*

- *Do you really want a relationship, or are you pursuing relationships because you think that's what you're supposed to do? Maybe you're just not interested in getting tied up. You know, unless it's the* right kind of *"tied up."*

Make a list of all the things you want in a partner. We focus too much on the things we don't want. "I don't want to meet someone who does this. I don't want someone who's just after my money. I don't want to meet someone who is unfaithful."

Switch it around. The Law of Attraction says you will attract what you think about, whether it's what you want, or what you don't want! Make a list of the traits you *want* in a partner. Figure out what is important to you. Compatibility? Kindness? Sex appeal? Good family? Loyalty? Spontaneity? As we get older, our lives get more complicated, and we get very stuck in our ways – that's okay – but you've got to find someone who fits into your life *OR* someone who can bring a new level to your life, like they take everything you've got and make it even better.

Try to move away from "tall, dark, handsome," or "hot, buxom, redhead." Look deeper into how you want this person to make you feel. How they improve your life. How they push you to become a better person. Are you going to bring value to their life? Are they going to bring value to yours?

### When Someone Breaks Up with You

I went through a breakup where I couldn't figure out what went wrong, and I couldn't get over it. I was depressed for so long. Life chugged on, and I felt utterly broken by this, and so hurt, and I beat myself up for such a long time. "What did I do wrong? What could I have done differently?"

What I finally realized, when that dark cloud lifted off me, was that there wasn't much I could have done differently. The timing was wrong. There were lessons that relationship needed to teach me. There was growth I needed to undertake. What had been my biggest heartbreak actual became my biggest blessing.

Finally what got me to move on was when I lost the sliver of hope…I was overthinking, constantly processing in my head. *Is he coming back? Can we try again? What can I do to make things right?* Unfortunately, that little sliver of hope, that crack in the doorway, prevented me from moving on.

Sometimes, you gotta kick that door shut. Throw a blanket over that sliver of hope and smother it. It doesn't sound easy – it's not easy – sometimes that sliver of hope feels like it's all that's keeping you going. Hope is a wonderful thing, but not in that form, not when it's keeping you stuck, digging yourself deeper and deeper into a hole. Hope should keep you striving forward, never keep you stuck in place. False hopes need to be put out of their misery. Forgive yourself, forgive them, and let it go. Cut the cord and healthfully move on.

Now I'm on an amazing, universal, God-given journey, and I trust in my Creator that everything is happening in his perfect timing. With that, I can relax and go with the flow. When I start to feel myself getting a little "Oh, do you think he'll call? Does he like me? Should I date him?" Once I start those questions, I realize it's not meant to be. When things are right, there aren't questions. My friends tell me, "When you meet the right person, everything is easy. It's seamless. You don't overthink or stress or worry about what you're saying."

Prepare to have your mind blown. Tunnel vision affects more than your career. It can keep you stuck in lousy friendships, lousy relationships, lousy situations of every type. Tunnel vision and attachment don't just happen to us in our careers. We can develop these feelings for any aspect of our lives.

For example, you might think, "I can only date handsome billionaire astronauts. I must have a white picket fence and 2.5 children."

The problem is, you cannot be attached to anything in life except yourself. You're the only person you can control. A friend of a friend recently had a really messy divorce. When she finally started dating again, she tried doing the "online" thing, and she got a fair number of first dates, but no second dates at all. Why not? Because she started every first date saying, "I'm looking for a serious relationship, and I'm not going to sleep with you until I know you're not just looking for sex," which was her sure-fire way to make her dates feel extremely self-conscious and wary. She managed to sabotage any potential fun, friendships, or opportunities because she was certain of two things: a) that she wanted nothing else but marriage, and b) that she was going to get hurt again. And it took her a very long time to come out of that vortex.

The romantic relationship is an area where I know I have my own work to do – and I'll continue learning, I'm sure. What I try to do right now is embrace my journey. I know that if it is meant to be, it will happen. If it doesn't happen, that's okay too. Relationships are everywhere around us. Beautiful relationships with friends, acquaintances, family members. Give yourself a break when it comes to "you gotta fall in love, get married, have kids, grow old together," because uh, no you don't. You don't gotta do jack shit.

Just be happy and be kind and go after what your heart desires, and don't force yourself into a situation that you're not comfortable in or not ready for just because you've "hit a certain age" or "all your friends are married." Go with the flow – if this particular event doesn't happen for you, that's okay – you're not "failing" at life.

## Summary

Relationships are the very stuff of life. No amount of money, nor houses, nor Ferraris, is really satisfying if you're lonely. Just remember a few things to lighten the fuck up about them.

- We put a lot of credit and energy into romantic relationships when there are plenty of other types we should nurture. Do not become so obsessed with romantic relationships that you neglect the other important relationships in your life. Falling in love feels wonderful, but that initial infatuation will evolve. Meanwhile, don't neglect **networking, friends, family, and your**

**community**.

- Do not force yourself into a romantic relationship out of a desire to conform to societal "norms." Don't settle – it's not fair to you, nor to the other person.

- Few things hurt more than romantic relationships coming to an end because we attach so much of our personal identity, and value, and even our future, to being a part of that couple. Try to remember that when a relationship does end, it is because it was not the right one for you. It is okay to hurt and grieve, but find value in the end, too. Find your way of letting it go as you learn from it.

# CHAPTER TEN

## TIME TO GET OUT OF YOUR OWN WAY

I have some sucky news. You're going to die.

Now you're thinking, "Wow, way to be a big bummer, Madison! Thanks for ending on a high note."

But as always, hear me out. I'm going to die too, and so is everyone else, but I look forward to seeing you all on the other side, because I believe in the afterlife. I don't think death is the end for us. But I do think that life on Earth matters tremendously, and that it is a wonderful opportunity that we should never neglect or waste.

I believe too, that in that afterlife, we'll all have a chance at some point to look back on the life we lived.

I certainly don't want to watch that movie of my life and see that I missed out on anything because I was standing in my own way. Here's the scene where I was too afraid to take a chance. Here's the scene where I was so obsessed with money that I refused to take the risks that would set me free. Here are the hours I spent worrying about cellulite. Here is the time I looked at a situation from the wrong perspective – uh-oh, there are a lot of scenes like that. Here is all the time I wasted feeling envious, angry, and offended. Here are the days I could have made life better just by being a little more chill and a little funnier.

Do you want regret to be part of your life's movie?

Now I don't want to be a big downer here, after all the fun we've had together, but if you haven't thought about this before, think about it now. Your life is passing *right now*. Are you making things happen, or are you still waiting for something else, for someone else, to get things started for you?

The things you want are there for the taking. Chances are good that if anything is stopping you…it's you. It's time to get out of your own way. I want you to remember these lessons that I've taken away from my own experiences, and use them to live your very best life.

Here we go!

### Stop overthinking everything.

This is just about the worst thing we do to ourselves. We worry about shit that will never happen. We worry about shit that is not important. We worry about shit that nobody notices.

You know, living your life is a lot like shaving your asshole. Overthink it, and you're likely to hurt yourself, pay too much, and wind up in therapy. Just give it a quick zip-zip with a razor, and there you have it – a nice, clean asshole.

Let's face it, most of our problems are self-made and easily resolved. Change your perspective. Be willing to walk away. Respect yourself and your value. Open your heart and mind to the fact that people are different everywhere, and let those minor irritations go.

## Enjoy your "right now."

This is so obvious, but we don't always do it. We don't let ourselves experience our "nows." We live for the weekend, for vacation, for holidays. We think about what we're doing later, what will happen when we get rich, get thin, or get married, and we ignore what's happening right in front of us. What if your happiest moments are the ones you're blowing off now? That's why my next point is...

## Your experiences today are memories tomorrow.

I remember my late twenties, early thirties, when I was living in the greatest city in the world. I was living my dream, doing stand-up comedy, I had great friends and a great social life. I looked good. Even back then when I was insecure, just trying to put one foot in front of the other, back when I was a total mess… now, I look back at all that like, "Wow, those were some of my best moments." All these amazing memories came back to me and I realized that every day and every moment is a memory and an opportunity, so make it count.

### Embrace sadness when you need to.

Don't hate yourself or regret the times when you slip up, when you feel sad or depressed - there are so many reasons why you might feel "down" for a while. This is a real emotion that is a real part of life, and fighting it is denying it's importance in your overall happiness. Have a long, hard, terrific cry. You will feel better and be able to move forward sooner.

### Time is your most valuable commodity.

You can't buy it. You can never get back. Don't waste it, not for yourself or others. Don't waste it standing in your own way!

### My Wishes for You

You've been given a great gift and all the tools you need to use it.

No, I'm not talking about this book! I mean, sure, this book is pretty awesome, but the gift is your *life*. I plan on using mine to its full, passionate potential. How about you?

Let's wrap it up in a way that's easy to remember:

- Look for opportunities everywhere.
- Listen to diversity of thought.
- Laugh at the things that try to slow you down.
- Let go of the shit that holds you back.
- Love the people who have been there for you.
- Live in the present.
- Lighten the fuck up!

Manifesting you all the best, until next time,

*Madison*

CPSIA information can be obtained
at www.ICGtesting.com
Printed in the USA
BVHW050241090123
655844BV00003B/260